I0450140

choosing the *right* domain name:

a marketing perspective

all you need to know about domain names

(and some you don't *need* to know,

but is interesting anyway)

ALAN CHARLESWORTH

For Beth

I hope your domain name is useful one day

CONTENTS

CHAPTER THREE

DOMAIN NAME CHOICE – GETTING IT *RIGHT*

CHAPTER FOUR

WHERE – AND HOW – TO SHOW OFF YOUR DOMAIN NAME

INTRODUCTION : WHY IS THE *RIGHT* DOMAIN NAME SO IMPORTANT?

My mum always told me that first impressions are lasting impressions. And she was right. In the click–away–in–an–instant world of the Internet, however, first impressions are more than lasting. They are critical.

For the potential customer, the first reference they have to an organization's online presence is its domain name. And its domain name may influence how a potential customer perceives that organization. That is: poor domain name = poor company, good domain name = good company to do business with. OK, so this might not be absolute – but given that a domain name costs so little, why not indulge customers' perceptions?

DOMAIN NAMES IN PRACTICE
you are your domain name

You see two ads on TV for companies offering financial services. One has the domain name **loans.co.uk** and the other **onecall.ws**. All other things being equal, which company carries most credibility?

Choosing an effective domain name is a crucial decision for any organization – and it is a *marketing* decision. It is not a decision be taken by members of staff who do not fully appreciate the value of a good domain name – or the shortcomings of a bad one.

A popular description of a domain name is that it is the organization's address on the Internet. Well, if you were a physician, would you rather ply your trade from: 1 Harley Street, London, or: flat 4B, (above the tattoo parlor) High St,

Anytown? The answer is, of course, Harley Street. More importantly, if you were looking for a doctor, wouldn't you choose the one in Harley Street? The truth is that this is nonsense. Why should a doctor in Harley Street be better than one based in a provincial town? And why should an organization with a *good* address be any better than an organization with a *poor* address? Surely it is the quality of the product or service that is important, not the supplier's address? But that's human nature for you, we are not always rational in our buying decision making. Offline, of course, that Harley Street address – or one like it – will cost you a small fortune. Online, the right domain name will cost you no more than a basic first aid kit.

DOMAIN NAMES IN PRACTICE

coffee is more important than a domain name

In a survey, FastHosts Internet found that the UK's small businesses are rushing their choice of web address. Apparently, 41% made the decision in less than an hour – around the same time they took to source their office's coffee making machine. This was despite most of them recognizing that their domain name could have a lasting effect on their business, with one third of owners believing that their revenue would improve as a direct result of having a better web address. More than 60% of respondents did not seek a second opinion, and only 10% of businesses considered the long term effect of their domain name on their business image. No surprise then, that many UK businesses believe their choice of domain could have been better.

To have a website, the organization must have a domain name. If you must have *a* domain name, then you should not just have a *good* domain name, you need the *right* domain name.

PREFACE

Many of the examples I use in the book are of organizations that are local to me in the UK. Don't be put off or disregard them if they are not from your part of the world. They are only illustrations. There will be similar examples of both good and bad practice from all around the world – including that part you are in. Furthermore, in Europe we have always had more suffixes/extensions to complicate the choice of domain name, so perhaps we have the edge in experience over our American compatriots?

I have divided the book into four distinct – though related – chapters, they are:

1 The who, what, where and when of domain names

If you are going to choose the *right* domain name then you need to know a bit about their history, construction, registration and the system in which they exist and are used.

2 The legal aspects of domain names

Don't skim past this section because the term 'legal' frightens or bores you. I'm not a lawyer, and I don't write 'legaleeze' – but you need to know (a) how not to break any laws when registering names, and (b) what to do if you are the innocent party in a domain name dispute – or better still, avoid getting into that position in the first place.

3 Domain name choice – getting it right

Perhaps the section most people will buy this book for – its title says it all – with advice on creating the *right* domain name for a whole range of different scenarios.

4   Where – and how – to show off your domain name

You might think this is a bit 'old hat' – but so many get it wrong. Read and learn.

These sections are designed to take you through the domain name selection process in chronological order from deciding you need a domain name through to promoting it to its target audience.

Throughout the book, unless circumstances dictate otherwise, domain names are presented without the 'www' eg atrustingbusiness.com rather than www.atrustingbusiness.com. This reflects the way in which domain names are referred to in general conversation – ever heard anyone say they bought something on www.amazon.com? Also, right through to the last chapter I present all example domain names in lower case – there is a reason for this, as you will find out in chapter 4.02.

I make no apology for not listing organizations that offer the types of services that I might mention in this book. There are a number of reasons for this, not least that:

I.   I want the content to be independent. When searching online for information on domain names, invariably the only place you will come across any advice is on the websites of companies that offer domain name–related services. To my mind this taints any advice they offer as it will inevitably steer the user towards the registration services favoured by that organization.

II.   Whilst I use some services offered by domain name–related companies (some free, others paid for), I do not want to recommend them. The reason is that there are hundreds of organizations around the world who offer similar services. If I recommend one, the inference is that the others are not as good – and I simply do not know if that is the case.

III.   Times change. I might recommend an organization that is good at the time of writing, but it might go downhill immediately afterwards. Or even go out of business. How good is a referral to a company whose website returns a '404 gone away' message?

It is also worth noting that when I have checked a domain name to see if there is a website hosted on it, I sometimes make the comment that there is no site – or the page returns a 'server not found'-type message. In all instances I repeated the request over a period of days to check that the non–response is not down to a temporary fault rather than a permanent state of affairs. Naturally, it is possible that I list a domain name as 'hosting no website' but by the time you read this text a site has been established on it. Conversely, a site that was live when I checked it might not exist by the time you see it featured in this book.

And finally for this section, although the basic premise of the advice offered in this book will remain constant over the coming years, some things will change. To address this, I will be maintaining an associated website where you can track any changes or updates to the chapters, you will find this on: alancharlesworth.eu/domain–names.

CHAPTER 1

the who, what, where and when of domain names

1.01 DOMAIN NAMES – WHAT'S THEIR HISTORY?

Every presence on the Internet is identified by a series of numbers (142.56.89.43, for example). This is called the Internet Protocol, or IP, address. To make these IP addresses easier to remember, the early proponents of the Internet decided to allocate a 'name' (or series of characters) to each IP number. Because no two sets of IP numbers are the same, no two domain names can be the same. As the Internet was developed in the USA, the Americans were first to set up an authority to allocate *names* to the IP numbers. Subsequently other countries set up their own authority.

DOMAIN NAMES IN PRACTICE

The first domain name to be registered was symbolics.com, assigned on March 15th 1985.

Domain names are, and always have been, allocated on a first-come-first-served basis. The majority of generic, one word domain names were registered in the early to mid 1990s. Many of these were registered by IT students who were amongst the first to use the Internet on a regular basis. It is the generic .com domains that many consider to be the *best*. It is also difficult to trademark a generic word, which means that *generic* domain names are the most valuable in the open market.

It is worth noting at this point that although a domain name is intangible, the person or entity that registers the name is legally the *owner* of that name. This situation is complex in that the owner of the name does not have total control over its use. Rather than calling them the owner, ICANN (see next section) uses the legal–sounding term 'rightful name holder'. To complicate the issue still further, the person who registers the name is not necessarily the owner. And herein lays a warning. Few businesses will register their domain name with the relevant naming authority, they will do so through a registrar – see section 1.06, *how to register a domain name*. When I registered the names that I *own*, I did so through a company that I trust. I trusted them to put me down as the owner, which they did, because I know how to check. Sadly I have come across a number of organizations that did not use such reliable registrars. Or, as is more often the case, they trusted their website developers to register the owner of the domain name as their client, not themselves.

The scenario is that A Trusting Business Ltd hires Dodgy Web Design Inc to develop a website, register a domain name and arrange the hosting of name and site. What Dodgy Web Design Inc does is register the domain name – atrustingbusiness.com – but lists themselves as the owners of the domain. To make matters worse, Dodgy Web Design pay for the hosting service in their name also. A few months down the road, A Trusting Business Ltd wants to make some changes to their website or becomes dissatisfied with Dodgy Web Design – and it is only then that they discover they have no access to their website or domain name. Although they might feel like sending a team of 'heavies' round to see their website developers, protracted legal action is probably the only recourse for A Trusting Business. And by this time A Trusting Business has had all of their stationery printed with the domain name (which they don't own) directing customers to their website (which they can't change). *And* it is also painted on the sides of their trucks and vans. Not the sort of situation you want to find yourself in.

DOMAIN NAMES IN PRACTICE
from the history books

In the early days of the world wide web – and I'm only talking about the mid–1990s – surfers had to type in the http:// at the beginning of any URL. Contemporary users are now relieved of this chore as browsers now add the http:// as a default when www is entered before the domain name. Whilst in 'those were the days' mode, early versions of the Internet Explorer browser defaulted to the .com of any given word. So back around 1998 simply typing 'atrustingbusiness' (no www, no http://, no .com) into the browser window and hitting the 'enter' button took you to http://www.atrustingbusiness.com. Although this state of affairs didn't last too long, it served to cement the value of .com over other suffix options.

Contemporary browsers commonly need only the primary domain and suffix to be entered in order to deliver a web page (eg atrustingbusiness.com), though entering only the primary name (eg atrustingbusiness – no www, no http://) returns whichever website is sitting at the top of the browser's associated search engine results for that term.

1.02 WHO RUNS THE SYSTEM?

The Internet Corporation for Assigned Names and Numbers (ICANN) is responsible for a range of technical aspects of the internet, including the co–ordination of the assignment of domain names. The Domain Name System (DNS) allows for the registration of domain names within a number of registries known as 'top level domains' (TLDs). TLDs fall into two broad categories:

- Generic top–level domains (gTLDs) eg .com

- Country code top–level domains (ccTLDs), such as .uk for the United Kingdom and .au for Australia.

DOMAIN NAMES IN PRACTICE

who is a domain name's owner?

The InterNIC (www.internic.net) is a registered service mark of the U.S. Department of Commerce and provides all you need to know about domain names with US extensions (suffixes). There is also a 'whois' section where you can check the details of who owns what for US extensions. Note however, that registrants can now opt-out of having their full detail made public, and that similar facilities have limited availability for European names as the information is covered by various data protection regulations.

Each country has its own *naming* authority which runs the domain name system for that country. For example, in the USA the regulating agency is the Internic (internic.net), the UK's ccTLD registry is owned and operated by Nominet UK (nic.uk), France's is AFNIC (nic.fr), Germany's DENIC (denic.de) and Canada's CIRA (cira.ca). The majority of these are not–for–profit companies or public sector organizations (eg universities). A full list of ccTLDs and their sponsoring organizations is available on the website of the Internet assigned numbers authority (IANA) – go to iana.org and follow the link on it's the homepage to 'database of Top Level Domains'.

To register a name you must apply to the relevant authority for 'permission' to use that name. It is rare, however, for a user to actually use the naming agencies directly, it being more likely that they will use intermediaries – 'registrars' (or 'registration agents') – to register their domain name. It is also the case that although you might *own* a domain name that agency retains the authority to withdraw it from use on the Internet – making it, effectively, useless. It is also worth noting that although you might have registered your domain name – and so own it – such is the system that if you don't renew its registration on an annual basis that registration expires and, eventually, the name is made available on the free market – often by auction. Although it is possible to pay these annual fees for years in advance, this can result in the renewal being

---

DOMAIN NAMES IN PRACTICE
expired domain names

Expired names can be valuable – enter the *drop catcher* who uses software to check on names that come back onto the market (around 20,000 a day) and registers any that might be valuable. Having taken ownership of the name they can; offer to sell it to the previous owner, auction it, perhaps to competitors of the original owner, or as the domain might have a high position on search engine rankings, use it to host a website loaded with ads, so earning significant income.

1.03 HOW IS A DOMAIN NAME CONSTRUCTED?

When a name is registered, it takes the suffix of the authorised naming authority for the relevant country. There are a number of suffixes to choose from (more of this later) but to help illustrate how domain names are constructed I am going to use the best known suffix – .com (dot com). Note that in the USA, the *suffix* is more commonly referred to as the *extension*. The domain used as an example is: atrustingbusiness.com.

As the suffix is considered to be the *primary*, or *top level* domain, combining the 'name' with the suffix creates a *second* level domain:

eg   atrustingbusiness.com

When indicating their use as the URL (Uniform Resource Locator) of a world wide website, it has become accepted protocol to use the prefix 'www' on the primary domain name:

eg   www.atrustingbusiness.com

As the .com suffix now has two distinct 'words' before it, this is now a *third* level domain name.

Any subsequent 'words' – or series of characters – placed in front of the primary name, but divided by a full stop, make the URL a fourth/fifth level domain name. You can have as many 'words' prior to the domain as you wish, in practice however, three or four is really the limit.

eg   www.springfield.atrustingbusiness.com

In my 'atrustingbusiness.com' example there is no subdomain on the Top Level Domain as it is not being used as a Country Code Top Level Domain (ccTLDs). However, for ccTLDs the 'cc' element adds another 'word' to the full domain name (the USA with its .com is lucky in this respect). The following diagram shows the make up of a domain on the .uk ccTLD.

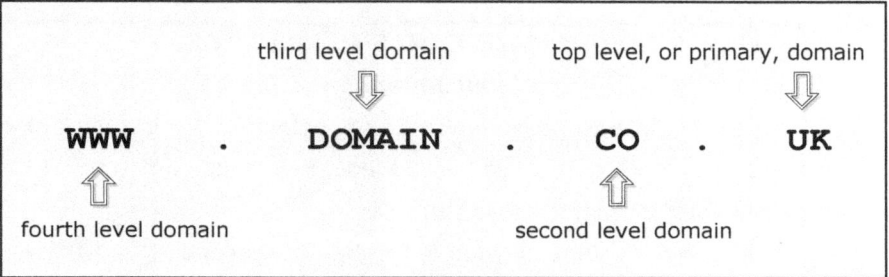

Note that multi–level domains are also referred to as 'subdomains', eg a third level *sub*domain. Whilst the use of third/fourth level subdomains is not unusual, nor is it common practice. Its use is normally instigated by the IT department, using the third level as an extension to the domain to provide extra space for website content – think of it as an extra directory in which to keep files on a PC. When used in this way it is common practice to omit the 'www'. This means that when the web page is live in a browser window the address will read [something like] http://springfield.atrustingbusiness.com. From a marketing perspective this is not good practice. It creates a confusing state of affairs for web surfers who have become accustomed to seeing a 'www' and not having to type in the http://.

To be fair to the IT people, third level sites are usually accessed only as links from the primary domain site, therefore the surfer will not be required to actually type the URL into the browser. When third level domains are generated at the behest of the marketing department the www should be retained. Marketers want websites to be visited, and for that to happen the website address should be as clear as possible (a good *general* rule for domain names, more of which later), eg www.springfield.atrustingbusiness.com

---

DOMAIN NAMES IN PRACTICE

it's all Japanese to me

An advert in a Sunday newspaper supplement for visiting Tokyo entitled 'totally Tokyo' included reference to the URL; www.tourism.metro.tokyo.jp/english/.

This is rather confusing for a number of reasons. The fifth level domain is unusual, the combination of words are not obvious (some might associate 'metro' with city transport), .jp is rarely used outside of Japan (most .jp websites are in Japanese) and the final '/' is unnecessary. Without looking back – tell me the URL of the website.

See, I told you it was confusing.

Only the registered 'owner' of the name on the primary (top level) name can add second and any subsequent level names. An effective application of third level addresses is to expand web presence without registering more primary domains whilst still retaining corporate identity. Google, for example, uses the following:

video.google.com	maps.google.com	groups.google.com
news.google.com	images.google.com	earth.google.com
code.google.com	directory.google.com	

If you have been concentrating so far you will realise

that any organization that is using a name based on domains such as .uk.com or .eu.com has a problem. Effectively, they have 'rented' the third level of a domain name owned by someone else. This means that they do not have legal ownership of, or control over, the name – that is retained by the owners of the primary domain. Such names are often referred to as 'pseudo–domains', an apt description. Think of it as renting a room in an office block. You might have a contract with the owner of the block with regards to your office, but if he decides to paint the building – or even sell it – you have no say in the matter.

DOMAIN NAMES IN PRACTICE

ding dong ... poor domain name calling

Cosmetics retailer, Avon Products Inc, have websites for every country in which they trade. The majority of these sites sit on the relevant country domain, avon.de for Germany and avon.es for Spain for example. In a few countries the domain name avoncosmetics is used eg avoncosmetics.gr. Presumably this is because local companies have first claim on the trading name 'avon'. So far so good, until you look at the UK site – which sits on avon.uk.com. Oh dear. Both avon.co.uk and avoncosmetics.co.uk have websites on them, but neither would appear to have a rightful claim on the domain as neither site uses Avon as any kind of trading name. As Avon Products would have a valid claim on both, I wonder why they are using the .uk.com, particularly as the company has obviously gone to great lengths to register appropriate names around the globe. Could it be that someone somewhere actually thinks that .uk.com is the international domain for the United Kingdom? I would think not, given that the company also use avonshop.co.uk.

1.04 WHAT CHARACTERS CAN YOU USE IN

A DOMAIN NAME?

There is an unambiguous limit to the characters that can be used in a domain name. They are: all the letters of the Latin alphabet (A to Z) plus any number (0 to 9) and a hyphen (–). No spaces or other characters are allowed in a domain name. Note, however, that these rules apply to domain names that use the English language. Others, known as *Internationalized Domain Names*, are available in different languages – these are covered in more detail in chapter 1.05. A domain name must begin and end with a letter or a number. Any amount of hyphens can be used, but must not be placed together. Domain names must be at least three and less than 63 characters in length (excluding suffixes).

> **DOMAIN NAMES IN PRACTICE**
> **say aaaaaa**
>
> Some combinations of characters are registered for a purpose – but because it doesn't cost *that* much money, many are registered as a joke. Apparently every sequence of the letter 'a' on the .com suffix has been registered right up to the maximum of 63. Yes, that's:
> aaaaaaaaaaaaaaaaaaaaaaaaaaaaaaaaaaaaaaaaaaaaaaaaaaaaaaaaaaaaaaa.com

Although two letter domains do exist, they are only allocated to organizations that can prove that they are universally recognized by a two character name. Hewlett Packard uses hp.com, for example, General Electric ge.com and UK communications giant O2 use o2.co.uk. Realistically, however, unless you are in the same league as these examples, you can forget two character domains. Even rarer – and less-available –

are single-character domain names. For example, z.com is owned by Nissan (it redirects to nissanusa.com/z), q.com is owned by Qwest (redirects to qwest.com), x.com is owned by PayPal labs and g.cn takes you to google.cn. Quite how these sneaked through I do not know – but do not get the idea that single character domains on the main suffixes are an option for you. However, the summer of 2009 saw .biz domains become available on single and two character options. Whilst I am not convinced that ac.biz is a good domain for me or anything similar effective for other organizations, I would make two points, (i) it may be an indication of what other suffixes might make available in the future, and (ii) maybe a new business, could develop a new brand might around a single character .biz name. Buyers, however, seem to share my doubts, with only 5 of the 36 available single-character names being taken up in the original release. The most significant of these being overstock.com who registered o.biz for a B2B-only version of their service (note, that is 'o' for overstock, though they have also – sensibly – registered 0.biz, ie zero.biz).

Certain words are not permitted to be registered. These are the so–called '7 filthy words' that US Network TV and radio companies won't broadcast[1]. This ruling originates from a court decision following a New York radio station's broadcast (in 1973) of a 12–minute monologue entitled 'Filthy Words' which had been recorded earlier by a satiric humorist called George Carlin. So outraged were listeners that the major TV and radio networks agreed a ban on the seven words that caused such offence (if you are now thinking that you have heard bad language on American TV shows you will find that those programmes – Sex and the City, for example – are broadcast on Home Box Office (HBO) and not *networked* channels). Whilst this ban is closely policed by domain authorities, sometimes the odd word sneaks through (an example is featured in chapter 2.02).

DOMAIN NAMES IN PRACTICE
to hyphen or not to hyphen

In the US hyphens are rarely used, 'all one word' being the norm. In the UK we are more accepting of the hyphen in a domain name. This is particularly true if the organization's offline name uses a hyphen; 'lo–cost rentals', for example.

Which is best? As a rule, I favour the 'all one word' approach, but there are examples where a hyphen works, so there must always be room for exceptions to that rule (see chapter 4.02 for more on this).

Of course, given the cost involved, the simple answer is to register your domain name with and without hyphens – then use one as your primary name and have the other redirect to it.

The maximum number of characters that can be used in a single domain name is restricted by the relevant naming authority. The majority of these (many do not actually declare any limitations on their web pages) follow the .com rule of up 63 characters before the suffix (note that the http:// and any second/third level names eg www, are not included as they are not part of the *actual* domain name). Domain names for commercial use should never reach this limit, though – as usual – there will always be exceptions to this rule. For

---

[1] For obvious reasons, I'll not list them here – if you can't guess them, simply type "7 filthy words" into a search engine.

example, the imaginatively named 'the longest list of the longest stuff at the longest domain name at long last' website – can be found on:

thelongestlistofthelongeststuffatthelongestdomainnameatlonglast.com – in this case using all 63 characters in the domain name reflects the content of the site.

Finally – and this is important for marketing reasons that will be covered later – domain names are NOT case sensitive. From a technically standpoint, it is possible to set up a website's host server so that it recognizes upper and lower case characters in a domain name – so making a domain case sensitive. However, I have never seen this practiced – it being the standard operating procedure to set them up as being non–case sensitive. I have even spoken to techies who do not realise it is even possible to have case sensitive domain names. The same applies to email addresses. Once again, the default is to set up the email address to be non–case sensitive – and though I have come across one case sensitive email address (at a University in Northern Ireland) – the practice is ubiquitous. Even so it comes as a surprise to many people that email addresses are not case sensitive – you must have heard something like 'yes my email address is alan.charlesworth@atrustingbusiness.com, that's *lower case* a–l–a–n ...'. Or maybe you have done it yourself? Still doing it? Not after you have read this you won't. Not really a domain name issue – but take this as an added bonus – whilst characters in a domain name are restricted, this is not the case in the before–the–@ element of an email address. Yes, I could have $1000!@alancharlesworth.eu – but it would be very confusing for users, and so is not a good idea.

1.05 WHAT SUFFIXES ARE AVAILABLE

As I stated previously, suffixes have geographic origins. Here are the options for America, the UK and the rest of the world.

DOMAIN NAMES IN PRACTICE

you say extension, I say suffix

In the USA and other regions of the world, the domain name *suffix* is commonly referred to as the *extension*.

The United States

Because they are not limited to registration by American organizations, US–originated domain names tend to be treated as *global* and not country–specific. The most common are:

* .com : designated as 'commercial company'

* .net : designated as 'commercial company – alternative'

Note that .com and .net are administered by VeriSign Inc

* .org : designated as 'non–profit organization'. Although originally this was not 'policed' (it is not unusual to find commercial websites on .org domains) when the Public Interest Registry (PIR) took over its administration in 2003 it pledged to meet the 'unique needs of non–commercial organizations'

Others domains exist but are restricted to the pertinent establishments, eg .gov (government office), .mil (military) and .edu (education). In existence as long as domain names have been around, but rarely used until its 're–launch' in 2002, is the America–only .us. It is now commonly used as a second level domain for the US states eg .fl.us for Florida.

In response to demands for new Top Level suffixes, the Internic introduced:

- .info : unrestricted use

- .aero : air transport industry

- .biz : businesses – unrestricted

- .coop : co–operatives

- .name : for individuals – mainly sold as second level domains on the most common surnames eg john.smith.name

- .museum : yes, for museums

- .mobi : for web content which has been designed specifically for downloading to a mobile device (note that the advent of new mobile browsers – such as that on the iPhone – have rendered this domain largely redundant)

- .pro : for which second level domains were made available on: .law.pro (law-related services), .cpa.pro (accountancy-related services) and .med.pro (health-related services). These are only available to organizations and individuals that qualify as a member of the relevant US professional bodies

- .travel : for organizations in the travel industry

- .jobs : for the recruitment industry

Three of the newer TLDs (.aero, .coop, and .museum) are so–called 'sponsored top level domains' (sTLDs) created for a particular industry sector and administered by a trade body or other representative group. It is likely that any future additions will be 'sponsored' – as is the case for the recently introduced .jobs.

Whilst .com is still far and away the most popular US suffix, with others being mainly frowned upon (for .biz, read poor substitute for .com), the lack of *good* available .com names will inevitably lead to examples of new suffixes becoming more common in years to come. For example, the suffix .xxx has been long muted for use on websites with adult material, but protests in the US congress stalled its progress and in May 2006 it was rejected – though experience still keeps nudging me to say it might not have gone away forever.

DOMAIN NAMES IN PRACTICE

dot biz is not the biz?

Around three quarters of registered .biz domain names have no websites on them and a quarter registered to the same organization that registered the corresponding .com (source: Harvard Law School, 2006). This would appear to make the whole .biz name something of a waste of time – except to those companies that make a profit handling the registrations.

At the time of writing, ICANN – having estimated that only 17% of the original four billion network addresses remained available, and that addresses are expected to run out within five years – put forward a suggestion for what might be the most revolutionary event in domain names to date. The proposal will allow companies to purchase new generic top–level domains ending in almost anything they wish – in particular, their brand name. So rather than me having alan.charlesworth.eu, I could have alan.charlesworth – with 'charlesworth' being the suffix. More realistic is that an organization like eBay would come up with the fee (touted as being anything from 25 to 250,000 dollars) then sell domains to their customers for use on eBay-linked websites – alanstoys.ebay, for example. Or Nike could have soccer.nike, tennis.nike, golf.nike and so on. Another possibility might be cities (though quite who – council, private company – would own/administer the domains would be problematic) using the suffix for businesses in each city, alansrestaurant.newyork perhaps. However, given the sums of venture capitalist's money poured into 'e' businesses since the birth of the Internet, perhaps some entrepreneurial types will see an opportunity to make money by selling names based on generic top–level domains? The following spring readily to mind: .news, .restaurants, .hotels and .books. Or what about .websites or .phonenumbers for some kind of online directory? Despite innovations in domain names having a history of protracted launches, this one is planned for introduction in 2010. I'm not holding my breath.

DOMAIN NAMES IN PRACTICE
effective use of dot info

An example of effective use of the .info suffix is the ariel.info website from Procter and Gamble. This is not a corporate website, but a source of information (for consumers) on washing clothes – an 'infomercial' if you will. There is a second lesson included here regarding the spelling of similar domain names. Note of the spelling of the washing powder. Everything you need to know about the *font* of the same name is on arial.info.

Another TLD that has been heavily promoted but seems to have had little take–up is the .me suffix. Originally planned to be for individual's websites it is, however, unrestricted. This means that for limited applications it does have *certain* originality – hire.me for a recruitment business or talkto.me for a communications company perhaps.

DOMAIN NAMES IN PRACTICE

the hardest-to-get suffix of them all?

The .int gTLD is reserved for international treaty–based organizations and United Nations agencies – a rather exclusive group, and so is perhaps the rarest of all top-level domains.

The United Kingdom

The second–level domains under the .uk ccTLD are:

- .co.uk : UK business, unrestricted – any person or business in the world can register

- .me.uk : Individuals, unrestricted – any person in the world can register

- .org.uk : not for profit organizations, unrestricted – any person or business in the world can register. The 'not for profit' element of this has never been 'policed', commercial websites can be found on .org.uk domains

- .plc.uk : UK Public Limited Companies, restricted – the domain name must be identical to the registered plc name

- .ltd.uk : UK Limited Companies, restricted – the domain name must be identical to the registered limited company name

- .net.uk : Internet network providers, restricted – though open to some flexibility. For example; doctors.net.uk seems to get round the rules by offering email services, or maybe it just slipped through the *net?*

- .sch.uk : UK schools, restricted

- .ac.uk : UK Higher Education establishments, restricted – though some HE-associated organizations are accepted eg hero.ac.uk

- .gov.uk : UK government departments, restricted

- .nhs.uk : UK National Health Service departments, restricted.

- .police.uk : UK Police forces, restricted

- .mod.uk : UK Ministry of Defense establishments or associated organizations, restricted

It is unlikely that even veteran surfers will have come across any of the following, but they are out there. Dating back to the early days of the web, all are still valid for the relevant organizations but rarely used. They are:

- .jet.uk : the Joint European Torus Project

- .aeatech.uk : AEA Harwell

- .bl.uk : the British Library

- .icnet.uk : Imperial Cancer

- .nel.uk : the National Engineering Laboratory

- .scot–off.uk : the Scottish Office

- .parliament.uk : UK parliament

- .nls.uk : the National Library of Scotland

Don't even think about trying to register a name on any of these.

The Rest of the World

There are over 250 countries with a country–specific domain, for example; .de for Germany, .jp for Japan, .fr for France, .ca for Canada and .gr for Greece. More than 80 countries are 'unrestricted' meaning anyone anywhere can register names. Some of these have been heavily promoted, but they are still considered as 'novelties' in the majority of business fields. These include .tv (Tuvalu) and .cc (Cocos Islands). The use of such domains is discussed in chapter 3.01.

Each country has made the decision as to whether they use second level domains in their suffixes. The one you will see most in this book is .co.uk – because I am from the UK. However, the UK is unique in its use of 'co' (we pronounce it 'coh', not see-oh) – most countries use 'com'. For example, businesses in Australia, Bahrain, Cyprus and Argentina use .com.au, .com.bh, .com.cy and .com.ar respectively. Others, like Canada, have opted to follow the US's lead and simply uses .ca as its suffix. Some countries, however, just like to make life complicated. Greek websites, for example, can be found on both .gr and .com.gr suffixes – and Mexico used only .com.mx for years before deciding to also allow registrations on .mx in September 2009. I'm not going to cover every country's options in this book – needless to say, if you are outside the US or UK you are likely to know your own country's options better than I.

DOMAIN NAMES IN PRACTICE
vive l'availability

June 2006 saw one of the bastions of restricted names fall. Previously available only to professionals, associations or public bodies, the French .fr registration was made available to any individual 18 or over and with a postal address in France. Les cybersquatters and Gaelic ne'er–do–wells must have rubbed there *mains* with glee.

As well as country specific suffixes that use Latin characters, there are also a growing number of Internationalised Domain Names (IDNs – also referred to as multi-lingual domain names) which use characters outside A–Z, 0–9 and the hyphen. At the time of writing around 40 additional character sets are available, supporting over 350 languages including Arabic, Hebrew, Korean, Russian and Greek. The registry responsible for operating each of the domain names or suffixes decides which, if any, additional characters can be used. For instance .com and .net are available in most major character sets including Arabic, Hebrew and Han (Chinese, Japanese, Korean ideographs). Many of the European suffixes, however, offer few non–Latin characters, in the main limiting options to accented letters – à, á, â etc.

Applications of IDNs for the marketer are limited. The most obvious issue is that if the domain uses non-Latin characters only the computer keyboards of users in countries where those characters are used can type in the domain name (OK, I know you could write the name by inserting characters from the PCs symbols file, but it is not very convenient). If an IDN is being used it is most likely the website will also be in the language of the IDN, so effectively restricting its use to geographic areas. For the marketer there are a few applications to consider:

- If your market is local to a region, you could gain brand value by using that region's language

- For a multinational company, websites for different countries could be in the language of each

- You might wish to appeal to expatriates in their native language

The problem with these suggestions is that, as with all forms of segmentation, you take the chance of alienating other potential customers by not using their language – or at least English, which is generally accepted as the world's *business* language.

The years 2006 and 2008 saw the launch of the long awaited .eu domain (it had been 'coming soon' since around 1998) and .asia respectively. Although the jury is still out, these domains (and other proposed regional TLDs) might eventually become a 'must have' for global traders based in those areas. It is worth noting that as registrants of .eu names must be registered by a person or company established in a European Union Member State, any transactions on .eu sites are subject to EU laws – something that might be attractive to potential online customers (see *domain names in practice* on page 20). However, given the shortage of available .com domains and the ever growing number of web users in Asia, the .asia in particular may prove increasingly popular – perhaps one day challenging the mighty .com for registration numbers?

DotAsia, the not–for–profit registry operator of the new domain was quick to spot an opportunity in the market by auctioning off some of the most popular generic names. It might be a reflection of trade in that region, certainly two, and arguably three, of the top six auctioned .asia domains were sex–industry related. The top six, with their purchase price at auction prices were:

1   discover.asia : $112,111

2   sex.asia : $83,334

3   buy.asia : $73,000

4   sexshop.asia : $53,607

5   gold.asia : $46,602

6   models.asia : $41,009

source: www.dotasia.org

1.06 HOW DO YOU REGISTER A DOMAIN NAME?

A S you need two named servers to register a domain direct with the naming authority, there are two main options when seeking to register a name:

1. Register it yourself using any one of the hundreds of online domain name 'registrars'. As with all services, quality and prices vary. If the service is *very* cheap there is probably a reason behind it. Choose a reputable organization. In the great scheme of marketing costs, even the most expensive are not exorbitant.

2. If professional services or consultants have been employed to develop your web presence, have the specialists register your name. Note however, that it is likely that they will simply use a registrar as described above.

Whichever you chose there is one vital issue to be aware of. Part of the registration process includes a section that requires details of the registrant – effectively who is the owner. Make sure that is listed as you (be that as an individual or organizational entity). It is not unknown for unscrupulous operators – both registrars and service providers – to list themselves and not their clients (see also chapter 1.01).

A further consideration is one of ignorance or unintentional action that has no malice but can be just as problematic. I have come across a number of examples where the employee tasked with registering a name has – innocently – listed themselves as owner. Several years down the line that employee has moved on – and you have a problem.

1.07 CAN YOU BUY A SECOND HAND DOMAIN NAME?

Yes you can. As previously stated, anyone who registers a domain name is, effectively, the *owner* of it. They can, therefore, pass on ownership to another person or entity for a fee. In chapter three we look in detail at how to choose the best domain name for your organization or venture – well it could be that the 'best' domain has already been registered by someone else. If this is the case it might be worth considering purchasing it from them – though if the domain hosts the website of a successful businesses or a recognized brand, it is unlikely to be for sale. However, as a business model, some people register names purely to sell them on, so those names will be available. Many other domains will sit between these two extremes – so depending on your budget, their availability might be worth exploring.

There are a number of websites that sell pre–registered names, though I have found these to be pretty much a waste of time. At the time of writing, for example, I could have purchased such gems as: decksterdecks.com, sellnmore.com, 1wsv.com and ckurhealth.com, all at the bargain price of $10 each – and they are over–priced at that I would say. Having said they offer little, it might be worth spending an hour or so trawling such sites – you are unlikely to find your primary name, but you may find something that is suitable for a particular element of your business or a name that describes your business but doesn't include your name. Either could be used on a microsite created to increase your online exposure, particularly for purposes of search engine optimization. An added attraction to pre-owned names is that (at the time of writing) Google takes into account the age of a domain name in its algorithms – meaning that an older name *might* appear higher in search results (note that there are many other elements to the Google algorithm).

If you do target a suitable, but already registered, domain, tracking down the owner of a registered name is your first job. Step one is to simply type the name into a browser. If a website appears, then the chance of buying the name becomes problematic. Not only is the owner unlikely to sell, but if you took over the name you would continue to receive the original site's traffic and, more importantly, you would have problems if the site has been indexed by search engines. If there is no website and the name is registered by a 'speculator' you are likely to get a generic website of the registrar with contact details for making a purchase. If no website appears this means that you need to track down the owner.

The details of who owns a domain name are made available through what is known as a *Whois* facility. These are provided by each Top level or Country Code organization – though they are available through many websites, normally those of domain registrars (to find a local Whois directory, simply put 'Whois' into a search engine). However, there is an obstacle for some domains – the data protection legislation that covers the country or region in which the domain originates. For an example, consider three of my domain names: alan–charlesworth.com, alancharlesworth.eu and alan–charlesworth.co.uk. For the first, registered in the USA, the Whois tells you who registered it (me) and my details, including my full home address. The second is managed by

Eurid, a European organization which is governed by EU Directives, and so their Whois tell you my name and a contact email address. The last one, the .co.uk, is covered by the UK Data Protection Act, which means you get my name and little else. It is worth noting, however, that reputable domain name registrars will offer a service – for a fee – of restricting the information on the US Whois facility, with the domain authorities being content for the data to be available from the registrars if it is required.

DOMAIN NAMES IN PRACTICE
keeping check on your competition

An extended use of any Whois facility is tracking domain name registrations to see what other players in your marketplace are up to. For example, the end of May 2006 saw the search giant register (through a not–too–difficult-to–identify third party) 'googlecheckout.com' – suggesting their future plans for diversification. Note that there are firms out there who will track your competitors' domain name activities – for a fee, of course.

For the vast majority of businesses, the purchase of an existing name is not really a serious consideration because for an existing company a suitable un–registered name is usually available, and for a new online venture the trading name of the business can be decided when availability of a suitable name has been checked However, if the circumstances are such that a suitable domain name has been identified as being for sale at a *reasonable* price then this is a effective path to follow. What is reasonable? It depends on what value the buyer places on the name – and how much the seller wants.

1.08 WHAT IS THE MONETARY VALUE OF

A DOMAIN NAME?

Like houses and second hand cars, domain names are not necessarily worth their sellers asking price. Their value is only what someone else is willing pay for them. Since the mid–1990s, individuals around the world have registered domain names in the belief that the names would be purchased, at great profit, by businesses eager to obtain a 'good' domain. In reality, few speculators have made much, if any, money by selling on names they have registered. Indeed, it is the lack of regular trading that has prevented any kind of market price being established for domain names. There are numerous websites that advertise domains for sale, but the prices are invented by the sellers. There is no benchmark or guide to fixing selling prices. Of course, many names do change hands, but for so little that the sales do not make the news – and for every domain name millionaire that does make the news, there are thousands of others who lose their investment.

One of the first examples I came across of buying the name of an existing company was in the 90s when the British Broadcasting Corporation – know universally as the BBC – purchased bbc.com from (if my memory serves) a US organization called Boston Business Computing for £213,000. That bbc.com is not currently used by the BBC is a mystery to me – it simply redirects to bbc.co.uk – but the answer probably lies in future online sales for the corporation.

Whilst the BBC example is a case of the seller 'having a price', other investors have made a profit by speculating on their – hopefully rising – value. Some pay substantial sums for names that they feel will appreciate in value of time. For example, men.com was purchased in 1999 for US$15,000, reselling in 2003 for US$1.32 million. Similarly, business.com must have seemed expensive when purchased in 1997 for US$150,000 – but that is nothing compared to the US$7.35 million profit made when it was sold on later. Other domain name sales of note include loans.com, which was purchased by the Bank of America for $3m, pizza.com for $2.6m, fly.com for $1.8m, seo.com for $5m, candy.com for $3 and Toys 'R' Us paid for $5m for toys.com. From a business point of view, such sums are a massive expenditure to recover *before* any other profits are made. From a marketing stand-point, however, if these names increase brand awareness, then increased sales – and profits – will be the result. Compare these sums, for example, with those paid to sports and movie stars to appear in just *one* promotional campaign – and even these domain names look to be a bargain.-

It is worth noting, however, that many of the domain names that sell for high sums have with them 'related assets' – normally functioning, profit-making websites complete with customer details – which is perhaps where the *actual* value lies. For example, a group of domain names including dictionary.com, reference.com and thesaurus.com were bought by Answers.com for $100 Million – but the websites hosted on those three domains were attracting 11.5 million unique visitors per month at the time the sale went through.

1.09 HOW CAN A DOMAIN NAME GENERATE INCOME?

Although I have included this section, it is not really what this book is about. Indeed, there are other books on this subject alone – you will find most of them under 'online get-rich–quick schemes'. Yes, some – a very few – people make money in the ways I am about to describe, but would I would advise it as a new business venture? Probably not. There are two distinct methods of generating incomes from domain names – *domaining* and *trading* – though, as you will see, the two are linked. Let's consider each in turn.

Domaining

This practice also goes by a number of other names, including *domain name parking* and *domaineering* – and is a descendant of an earlier incarnation, *cybersquatting*. Although still a popular term in the offline media, the original concept of cybersquatting was founded on registering names with a view to selling them to legitimate owners. As the courts got to grips with this practice it evolved into *domaining*, which can be divided into the legitimate and the not–so–legitimate. The success of early cybersquatting was based around the practice of 'direct navigation', but domaining has spun off into search engine optimization and pay per click (PPC) advertising – the latter being made possible by the emergence, and subsequent market dominance, of Google and its AdSense service.

Direct navigation is where a user types a web address directly into their browser – but doesn't get the spelling right. In the original – and not–so–legitimate – practice of taking advantage of this, practitioners register domain names which are similar to those of existing brands or websites. This might include such things as misspellings, typos, lookalikes, transposed letters, phonetic spellings and related stems – or even just a different suffix. Not that I am a famous brand but, for example, alancharlesworth could come out as: allancharlesworth, alancharlsworth, alancharlesw0rth or alancgarlesworth (try typing a few similar variations of well–known brands into your browser and see what you get). So now there are folk arriving on a fake site instead of their intended destination. As the early practitioners of the concept were usually in the adult industry, miss-typers were inevitably presented with pornographic images and promotions.

DOMAIN NAMES IN PRACTICE
the 'uk' can make all the difference

In the UK the .org.uk suffix is used almost exclusively by not-for-profit organizations. This means that *hi-jackings* on those domains have resulted in significant embarrassment for some organizations. What the hi-jackers do – and they are virtually all in the sex industry – is simply register the US .org version of the UK registration. The UK charity the National Deaf Children's Society, for example, found that when visitors to their domain – ndcs.org.uk – missed off the '.uk' they were taken to the **n**ude **d**ames **c**hat **s**ex website. Given the nature of the UK site, this hi-jacking was particularly distasteful.

Whilst this produced some income for the adult websites, most users simply clicked away as fast as they could. So the domainers moved with the times, and made the landing pages into sites that resembled the original destination domains – with content related to the mimicked site. However – and here is the money-maker – much of that content must be, or include, pay per click (PPC) ads. Effectively, each page is turned into what some describe as 'web billboards' – with the hope that each 'duped' visitor will click on at least one of those PPC ads before they go looking for the site they wanted in the first place. Just to make sure your have the gist of this **con**cept, here's a scenario. I need to buy a birthday present for my young niece, and she has professed an interest in a figurine of a character from the latest Disney blockbuster. So I head for the Disney website, but type in disneu.com by mistake. Up comes a webpage with Disney*esque* images and content and a banner that says 'buy your Disney movie character dolls online now'. The link may take me to the genuine Disney store or any other online retailer selling Disney character figures, but as I click on the link *kerrrrching* – the domainer has just added the clickthrough fee to their bank account.

OK, you say no harm, no foul – but there is. I've been conned. I wanted Disney, I got something else – and the Disney brand has lost out too. Also, the advertiser is paying for a clickthrough that was achieved in a dubious manner (though I might spend money on the site, I might also believe they were in on the con trick). Think of it as the guy selling knock-off 'branded' goods from a suitcase in the mall – that is, the mall paid for by the rents of *legitimate* traders.

However, so successful – read *profitable* – were these 'direct navigation' sites that the domainers soon realised the value of generic domains in this application. They would register a generic phrase – let's say taxreturnadvice.com – then simply list a whole host of PPC ads on the page and wait for the PPC commissions to role in (many of these sites take on the look – to the innocent user – of a shopping comparison site). Now this is where the search engines come into the equation. Without I go into too much detail on search engine optimization (it can get complicated) the content of these generic-word PPC-ad sites are attractive to the search engine algorithms, and so they appear at the top of the search engine results pages (SERPs). This means that if I typed "tax return advice" into Google, I could be presented with taxreturnadvice.com at the top of the list. Naturally, I go to the page, and ultimately click on at least one PPC ad.

DOMAIN NAMES IN PRACTICE
evil domaining

The most unsavoury method of making money by diverting 'innocent' surfers to a website they didn't intend to be on is where the pornography industry is involved. In March 2004 John Zuccarini, a notorious cybersquatter, received a 30 month jail sentence after becoming the first person to be found guilty of violating the US Truth in Domain Names Act. On several occasions, Zuccarini attempted to lure Internet users to a child pornography site through his use of misleading domain names. He used misspellings of domain names like Disneyland and Teletubbies to lure children to pornographic websites. Domain names that he registered included: dinseyland.com, bobthebiulder.com and teltubies.com, as well as 16 variations of the legitimate site operated by pop star Britney Spears.

So, where's the money in domaining? you might ask. Well, let's say 10% of visitors to my generic-domain website click on a single link, and each PPC averages ten cents. And let's suppose I get 100 visitors a day. That's a dollar a day. OK, Hardly retire-early-to-the-Bahamas income – but what if I had

1000 such sites? Or 10,000? Or 100,000? Or a million? – I'll let you do the arithmetic. A warning before you place that order for a new Mercedes, however. I said earlier that this is often the model presented by dubious 'get-rich-quick' schemes – and here's why. Do you really think there are any 'good' misspelled or mistyped brand names out there that haven't yet been registered as domain names? I'm afraid you missed this particular gravy train by a number of years – unless you have a bank balance big enough to allow you to buy some good generic names.

Furthermore, the income stream might be drying up – the result of a paradoxical problem for Google. As the dominant player in both search and online advertising, Google makes money from the PPC ads on the domaining sites, but at the same time searchers are increasingly unhappy at finding domaining sites at the top of the SERPs. Google's business model is based on giving users the best search experience possible, and the domainers impinge on this. If I want advice on completing a tax return and I search on Google for that term, I want web pages that will meet my needs – not a page full of adverts. In other words, I am annoyed with Google for returning a page that does not meet my search needs. Ultimately, if the search engine does not filter out (or de–list) these sites, I will take my search business to an engine that has. Of course, Google has recognized this and is taking steps to render the practice pointless by de-listing domaining sites.

As I said at the beginning of this section, there are a small number of individuals that are thriving on domaining – many pursuing the 'legitimate' route of PPC ads. There are, undoubtedly, other folk who are generating *some* income from lesser domain names. There are also people who make money by selling domains to these people (see the next section). Indeed, given that there are websites devoted to domaining as well as those that sell domains, there is a reasonable argument that this is a bona fide industry. For those folk who believe their fortunes lie in this field then I hope this book helps you to register or buy the right domain names. (If you want to know more about this business, simply type "Kevin Ham" into a search engine.)

Domain name trading

If you bought my book for this section alone then consider its purchase price to be to be an investment in saving yourself a lot of time, effort and money. Why? Unless you can time-transport your way back to 1994, you have missed the boat – for that's when all the good domain names (read: valuable) were registered. Yes, that man/woman at the pub/club/water cooler will always know someone (who knows someone) who has made a fortune by registering a name for 10 dollars and selling in for millions. But in reality these people are *very* few and far between. Doubt my word? Take a look at some of the pages and pages of ads on the 'domains for sale' sites I mention in chapter one. Yes, they've all been registered to make a fast buck but they are all still listed up there for sale – putting their sellers in negative equity for each one that remains unsold. OK, I will accept that there may be that one-in-several-million chance that the domain name you registered years ago *might* just be chosen as the new name for a global corporation that is re-branding itself, and one day their lawyers ring you up and make you a life-changing offer. But then your lottery number might also come up – the odds are around the same.

However, if you have a domain name or two, or two hundred, or two thousand and you don't want to follow the domaining route (let's face it, the vast majority of domains would attract zero visitors) perhaps you could sell them on to domainers.

You might even speculate on the domain name market, buying names that you hope will rise in value for resale – or attract visitors – at a later date. Some might argue that you can try to stay one step ahead of the market by tracking the business environment and registering domain names that mean nothing now but might come into vogue in years to come. The whole 'green' environmental issue might be an example. Or more recently, the announcement by the governments of various countries that they would pay owners to trade in old cars for new meant that a domain name with the words car or auto scrappage in them may have presented opportunities for fast moving domainers. However, such speculative practice requires both time and resources, making buying–to–sell domains virtually a full-time occupation – and a couple of hundred dollars return here and there will not pay the mortgage.

So there you go. Like a lot of similar industries, a few make a fortune. Most don't. You pay your money, you take your chance.

1.10 ARE MULTIPLE REGISTRATIONS WORTHWHILE? (1) Preventing Misuse

Are multiple registrations worthwhile to prevent misuse by others?

Yes.

Read the previous section and see what might happen if you simply register yourcompanyname.com. Plus, as well as those described who want be parasites on your brand, don't forget competitors who might leech on your success and those folk who – for whatever reason – wish to do your brand or organization harm by putting malicious content on a domain name that is similar to yours.

So multiple registrations are worthwhile to prevent misuse by others? Well ... no, not always.

For the seriously paranoid, the list of names that might be a misrepresentation of your name or brand is endless. Even taking into account the relatively low cost of domain names, this can become a serious financial – and resource-sapping – exercise. You can always register the most obvious examples – but beware, drawing the line between 'must register' and 'not worth it' can be extremely tricky.

My advice would be this:

- If you are an offline trader that uses a website for promotional purposes forget the whole thing beyond registering the local and/or .com suffixes.

- If you have an e-commerce site (ie you sell things online), consider registering any domain names on which a competitor might set up a site to 'steal' customers from you.

- If you are a global brand; register everything you can think of

Note, however – before you run off and register dozens of duplicate names, check out the next chapter on the legal aspects of domain names.

DOMAIN NAMES IN PRACTICE
know where to draw the line

The major brands and brand owners often register not only multiple spellings of those brands, but all suffixes of those names as well. This might add up to hundreds of domain names, but in the great scheme of marketing budgets, the cost is not significant. Having said that, it can be difficult knowing when to stop. With a bit of imagination it is quite easy to come up with dozens of variations on just the textual element of the name without multiplying them all by the number of suffix variants.

If you want to work on an example yourself, consider the Hilton hotel chain. To get you started, consider just the capital of the UK: londonhilton, hilton–london, london–hilton, hiltonlondon, thelondonhilton, thehilton–london, thelondon–hilton, thehiltonlondon. Did I mention there are three Hilton hotels in London? And according to their website, Hilton has three thousand hotels in 8o countries. Are you beginning to get the picture? And don't forget that you may want to register all of these on a number of suffixes.

1.11 ARE MULTIPLE REGISTRATIONS WORTHWHILE? (2) Strategic Applications

Whilst the previous section covers multiple domain name registrations for the same organization, product or brand, this element considers how the organization can use multiple domain names on a number of websites. Before I go into detail on this issue, however, it is important to emphasize that domain name policy is a *strategic* decision in that it is an important aspect of any integrated marketing efforts. Too often, companies – and I include some global brands – have no domain name strategy or policy, and as a result their websites are sitting on a mishmash of different domains and suffixes. For many, the best plan is to simply host all of the sites on one domain, with sensible use of second level domains and sub-directories. For the offline business using the web as part of its marketing efforts it is rarely worthwhile to register more than one domain name, except perhaps registering local and global .com suffixes for a domain (the additional cost is negligible). Another reasonable idea would be to have a generic name that describes the product or service offered and another domain that represents the actual name of the organization. Each domain could 'point' to the same website, or 'product' and 'corporate' websites could be developed for respective names. For example, UK retailer Boots have boots.com as their online store and boots–plc.com as their corporate site.

There are a number of aspects we need to consider when looking at multiple registrations for strategic purposes, they are:

- Organizations registering more than one domain name for multiple web presences. This can work if your products or services are aimed at different segments – allowing websites to be developed to appeal to specific markets.

- Organizations having a portfolio of names for use in, or registering them for, specific marketing campaigns

- Organizations registering names for some or all of the products they make or sell with the intention of developing microsites on them – this might be used to gain higher rankings on search engines (see also the next section on search engine considerations when choosing a domain name)

DOMAIN NAMES IN PRACTICE

redirecting (also known as pointing)

This is the practice where a domain name is set up so that if a user types it into a browser they are automatically taken – *redirected* – to another domain. For example, if you type boots.co.uk into your browser, the site that opens is on boots.com. Effectively, the alternatives to the primary name (misspellings etc) are 'parked' on a web server and when they are requested they 'point' the user to the main site.

In itself, the concept of pointing is not a problem – however there is an issue with *how* they are redirected. The problem stems from the technical side of things, namely 'server headers'. Server headers are a part of the system which tells the browser how to deal with a site. When the browser requests a site, they also receive a header code which tells them if the site is OK – a '200' return. Each possible outcome is given a similar header code – you will have come across the '404' return for 'no site found'. If the domain name is being redirected it is assigned

---

either a 301 or 302 code. The best option is to place 301 redirects on all domains. With this header code the surfer is taken directly to the website content of the main domain name. A 302, on the other hand, takes the content of the primary site and 'mirrors' it on the secondary domain. The user does not see any difference between a 301 and 302. The key issue lies with how search engines view each header code. When a search engine spider comes across a 301 it is redirected to the primary site, which it will then index. No problem. But when it comes across a 302 it reads it as a 200 because the content has been lifted from the primary domain and placed on that of the secondary. In other words, it reads it as a completely different site and will index it as such. This creates a problem for search engine optimization because when the search engine receives the 200 code it assumes it is OK to index all the pages, which is does. The search engine then recognizes that this is actually duplicate content (which it is – the only difference is the domain name). Duplication of content is frowned upon by search engines – they see it as a kind of spam – and they could take action against one or all of the domains up to and including banning them all from the index. This is particularly true if the organization has dozens, or hundreds, of domains all pointing at the same website.

Throughout this book I use the *domain names in practice* boxes to show examples of good and bad practice. In this section, however, rather than listing a whole load of potential scenarios, I offer a brief analysis of a series of strategic applications of domain name registrations as examples of practice.

The BBC From the early days of the Internet, the BBC has been astute in the way they have used it as a medium of communications – and this includes their use of domain names. In the following examples, all of the websites are part of the British Broadcasting Corporation – but all appeal to visitors from different markets:

bbc.co.uk	The main website
bbcworld.com	Global news highlights and headlines
bbcworldwide.com	A global 'corporate' site
bbcamerica.com	TV schedules and comment for shows aired in the US and available on itunes
bbcprime.com	As above, but for all other countries in the world
bbcmotiongallery.com	Access to thousands of shots from the vast and diverse archives of the BBC and CBS News.
bbctraining.com	The corporation's training and development department
bbcmusicmagazine.com	The world's best-selling classical music magazine
bbcresources.com	The site for the BBC's outsourced services centre in London
bbclanguages.com	Language courses for learners around the world

Suzuki   If the BBC's domain name policy suggests some joined–up thinking has taken place, Suzuki UK's is the opposite. What happens if you type suzuki.co.uk into your browser? Well, you get the 'home' page for the various Suzuki products, namely 'automobile', 'motorcycle' 'ATV' and 'marine' (as this book is about domain names and not website design I'll ignore the fact that in the UK we call them cars – not automobiles). Clicking on the links takes you to the following domains:

Automobile	suzuki4.co.uk (yes, I have typed that correctly – the relevance of the '4' is a mystery to me)
Motorcycle	suzuki–gb.co.uk
ATV	quadrunner.co.uk
Marine	suzukimarine.co.uk

Calling this domain name strategy a shambles is being unkind to shambles around the world. The marine offering is the only one that makes any sense – so why not have 'suzukicars' (registered by a suzuki car dealership), 'suzukimotorcyles' (available) and 'suzukiatv' (registered, but not by Suzuki GB)[2]. Apart from (a) the obvious confusion for customer, and (b) the unprofessional brand image presented, there is also the obvious opportunity for 'squatters' to register names that take advantage of the situation (take a look at suzuki1.co.uk, for example), so reducing the brand value still further. But this story doesn't end there. The American Suzuki Motor Corporation use suzuki.com as the 'home' page – with the links going to:

Automobile	suzukiauto.com
Motorcycle	suzukicycles.com > then suzukicycles.com/Product Lines/Cycles.aspx

---

[2] These standings correct as of June 2009.

ATV	suzukicycles.com > then
	suzukicycles.com/Product Lines/ATVs.aspx
Marine	suzukimarine.com

I also did a quick check on a number of other ccTLDs for 'Suzuki' and the shambles is rife around the globe – even Suzuki.asia has been registered by a domainer! Now, I do appreciate that the various outposts of the Suzuki empire might be different business entities – but, hey, they are all part of the global brand that is Suzuki – can't someone in Japan get their various acts together?

Yes Car Credit   Although their overall business practices can't have been too good (the company ceased trading in 2005), at least Direct Auto Finance Ltd had given some thought to their use of domain names. The company traded as Yes Car Credit, with yescarcredit.com hosting their website and the .co.uk version redirecting to the .com. So why was yescarcredit.net featured on their TV adverts? What about the .com or .co.uk, after all, they are the most commonly recognized suffixes in the UK? I would suggest that it allowed the company to measure the success of their TV advertising. Any surfer who arrives at the site via a .net URL will (almost certainly) have seen the TV advert. Promotions in other media could use the .com or .co.uk and so help determine the ROI of those promotions. Some may argue that the range of domain names might confuse users. I would say this is not a problem, because as the company had registered (and used) all the popular names, the potential customer would arrive on the Yes Car Credit website whatever suffix they use. The additional cost incurred by the marketers of Direct Auto Finance Ltd for this creative use of domains would have been a drop in the ocean that was their overall marketing budget – and definitely not enough to send them into administration!

DOMAIN NAMES IN PRACTICE
domain name crime?

Is it *irony* when a 'crime stoppers' website has its domain name stolen from under its nose? Only a few hours after the crimestoppers-uk.org (note the hyphen) website was launched in a blaze of publicity, crimestoppersuk.org was registered by someone else. Not a crime to register the name, of course – but whoever at Crime Stoppers UK that was responsible for not registering both versions committed a serious online marketing offence.

Newcastle airport   An example of lack of forethought in registering names comes from my local airport. The website is found on newcastleairport.com, which I can live with – it's what people call it, even though its actual name is Newcastle *International* Airport. It is also the case that newcastleinternational.co.uk, newcastle–airport.co.uk and newcastleairport.com all redirect to the main domain. On the downside, however, newcastleairport.co.uk redirects you to ourports.com – a company that deals with transport to, and parking and accommodation at, airports. Also, newcastleinternational.com takes users to a domainers page of a company in Las Vegas. My opinion? Ourports and the domainer are being a bit naughty registering the name, and I would have thought that Newcastle Airport would win any ownership contest. On the other hand, from a sales point of view, full marks to Ourports, and shame on you Newcastle Airport for not registering the .co.uk and .com. versions of your domain names.

Procter and Gamble   They are one of the world's biggest spenders when it comes to marketing, so P&G's use of domain names is worth a closer look. On the positive side, they are reputed to be the owners one of the world's most extensive collection of domain names, including not only various suffixes of their brand names, but many generic words that might be connected to their product ranges. However, if they were quick to spot the advantages that could be gained from the innovative use of domain names, they do not fare so well with their own name.

Procter and Gamble operate on the web as their global brand identity of P&G by using pg.com. To find details of P&G's local operations you must access pg.com and select the relevant geographic region or country – and it is the domains on which these sit that cause me concern. The first ones I looked at were around Europe, where several third level domains are used. For example, France is fr.pg.com, the UK uk.pg.com and Germany .de.pg.com. I think this is sensible – but P&G are not consistent. Greece, for example, is p–g.gr and Hungary, pg.hu – whilst further afield, the site for India uses pg.com/india.

I can't help but think that this could be handled a whole lot more effectively, but it is also the case that this is a website architecture and management issue as much as it is a domain name dilemma. An obvious problem with any domain name policy is whether the same model can be used around the globe – something that is particularly relevant for P&G in that they have opted for a two-character brand-name derived domain name. This is because many countries stick to the minimum-three-character rule – so 'pg' is not an option in those countries. Another advantage of sticking to third level names is that P&G have total control over the names and the sites that sit on them as they all defer back to the pg.com 'parent'. This would mean they need not worry about domain name decisions made by smaller countries that might impact on their various web presences.

Domain name management   Whilst   there   will   be circumstances when multiple registrations are a good idea or business strategy, there is still the issue of *managing* them. For the SME with half a dozen it is not a significant issue – though someone should be made responsible for them. For others,   like   my   Hilton   Hotels   example,   domain   name management   is   either   a   full-time   job   or   something   you outsource to a trusted third party – if only to ensure their annual registration is kept up to date. Don't dismiss this lightly – both Microsoft and Amazon have been guilty of letting domain names lapse in the past.

1.12 WHAT SEARCH ENGINE CONSIDERATIONS ARE THERE WHEN CHOOSING A DOMAIN NAME?

As far as search engines are concerned, domain names impact in two ways: the search algorithm and the search engine results page (SERP), so let's consider each in turn.

The search algorithm

As this book is about domain names and not search engines, I'll not spend too long trying to explain what a search engine algorithm is and how it works. However, just so you have some idea (if you don't already), here's a *very* rough guide.

The Algorithm is the set of rules by which a search engine ranks the websites listed in its index in relation to a particular query. No one really knows the exact details of each algorithm as they are kept secret by the search engines. Imagine it as a kind of points–allocation system where each web page is assessed against certain criteria and awarded points for each. The web page with the highest points total is the one that is listed at the top of the SERP. However, the points allocation varies from element to element – so some factors earn more points than others. Naturally, all businesses want to be at the top of the SERP if a user searches on a keyword or term that is associated with the product or service they are selling – so optimizing your web pages in order that the search engine's criteria are met is an essential part of online marketing. This discipline is known as search engine optimization (SEO). Part of the algorithm (Google's is said to have around 200 different factors) aims to match the term used by the searcher – the keywords – with the use of that term within the web page's content and its programming code. It is a logical conclusion, therefore, that if the website's domain name includes the search term then that would indicate that the website has content on that subject. If you searched on my name (as keywords) you would expect alancharlesworth.eu to have some connection with someone called Alan Charlesworth, for example. Although I have used my name as an illustration, perhaps more pertinent is the use of generic terms in domain names – loans.com being about borrowing money and toys.com about children's play-things, for example. Although the search engine's algorithm is secret, my views on the SEO value of having keywords in the domain name are shared by many experts – a panel of 72 SEO experts who contributed to the 2009 Search *Engine Ranking Factors Report* rated 'having the keyword in the domain name' as #3 in on-page ranking factors.[3]

Another part of the algorithm is to look at the *reputation* of the domain on which the content sits. This 'domain strength' includes:

- Registration history, ie multiple or single owners

- Domain age – when was it (a) first registered, and (b) used

- Has it been used continuously since it was registered?

What the search engines are trying to do is establish the validity of the web page to which they are sending their customers (searchers) – the concept being that a domain name that has had only one owner and a website on it for 15 years is

---

[3] Many commentators think the August 2009 Google 'caffeine' update gave more SEO weight to having keywords in a domain name.

more likely to be a reputable site than one sitting on a domain name that was registered only a couple of weeks ago. Think of it as checking on the provenance of an antique.

Although the value of a search term being within a domain name might be open to debate – what is undisputable is the impact of the suffix. Perhaps not fully appreciated by those Americans who have not left their own shores, is that in the rest of the world the major search engines allow users to search 'the web' (ie the world) or 'local' (eg pages from Canada) … and in the latter, local suffixes are given priority. For example, my own website – which is on a .eu suffix – is top of the Google 'global' search for my name – but if I search on 'UK only', the site is on page five or six. This is the reason for my registering alan-charlesworth.co.uk – that web page is top of the 'UK' results.[4]

DOMAIN NAMES IN PRACTICE

checking a domain name's past

A 'Whois' look-up might help with registration history, but you could also try the 'way back machine' on archive.org. It will show you web pages that have been hosted on domains in years gone by – so you can see if your desired domain name has had a previous life as a XXX porn portal. Note that such checks are advisable not only for purchasing 'second-hand' names, but any registered as 'new' – the name may have been allowed to lapse by its previous owners and have been recycled into the system.

---

[4] Note that Google have a 'geotargeting' tool that domain owners can use to set their domain's geographic target for users who are using 'local' search, and also that many commentators suspect Google already presents 'local' results higher in SERPs, but this is based on the location of the searcher's IP address.

Still on the subject of search engines and suffixes, some commentators suggest that the .info is not liked by the engines. This may be true, but note that where I recommend a .info as an option for a website it is normally the case that high SERP listings for that site are not a priority.

I will conclude this section with a caveat. The search engine companies and their algorithms are a law unto themselves. The factors I have raised represent a consensus of opinion in SEO circles – but these factors may or may not *actually* be an element of the search engine's algorithm.

Not only do the experts fail to agree on the specific composition of algorithms, but those algorithms change periodically – adding to the uncertainty.

The search engine results page (SERP)

A constant in any aspect of marketing is the importance of customer perceptions. What this means – effectively – is that it doesn't matter what we (the sellers) think of our product, what is important is how customers *perceive* our product. It is this concept that comes into play with regard to the SERP – the page that comes up when you instigate a search on, for example, Google.

When a user searches on a keyword, the SERP lists the top ten matches, each of which *seems* to meet the criteria of the searcher. There ends the role of the search engine algorithm – though its last action is to hi-light in bold the search term wherever it appears on the SERP. The searcher must now choose which of the results they wish to click on. Practice suggests that the top one is always favourite, but how can the domain name of the featured sites influence the searcher? Could it be that, faced with 10 site listings that all seem to say the same thing, I might be drawn to click on a website where the domain name reflects the search term (ie my motive for performing the search) – and don't forget it will be bold. For example; I am looking to buy a genuine ex-army parka jacket, so I type "ex-army parka" into Google. Up comes the SERP listing 10 sites that all sell military surplus products – might the site with the domain **ex-armyparkas**.com showing in bold appeal to me more than alanscoats.com – even though both may carry the same stock and sell it at the same price?

DOMAIN NAMES IN PRACTICE
generic domains in SERPs

The first page of the Google search on "fancy dress" returned links to sites including (bolded as per the SERP):

buycostumes.com	letspartynow.co.uk
all**fancydress**.com	wonderlandparty.co.uk
ace**fancydress**.co.uk	escapade.co.uk
dreamers**fancydress**.co.uk	partydomain.co.uk
simply**fancydress**.co.uk	

But none of these are as good as that of Angels Fancy Dress: **fancydress**.com.

The same company also has fancydress.co.uk (which redirects to the .com) and I would guess that the reason these folk registered the best name in that market is because they have been *'supplying costumes to the entertainment industry for over 165 years'* and they saw the potential of the Internet – and so registered the name in the early days of the domain name gold rush. Full marks for that.

Of course, it is just perception, but – all other things being equal – doesn't the website with the domain name which includes the product I am looking for seem more attractive?

And remember, 'online, the competition is only a click away' – and nowhere is that more true than on the search engine results page.

1.13 BEYOND THE DOMAIN NAME – GOOD PRACTICE IN URL CONSTRUCTION

It might be a reasonable argument that this section is not actually about domain names because a domain name *can* be a URL but a URL is not necessarily a domain name. For example, www.alancharlesworth.eu is both a domain name and a URL. www.alancharlesworth.eu/contact.html is a URL but it is not a domain name. However, as domain names and URLs are inextricably linked, I've included this section because it has relevance to some aspects of domain name use.

For most techies and programmers, directory and file names are just something they use to segregate one from another – hence you get URLs that are full of numbers, question marks, tildes (that squiggly thing '~') and heroes from their favourite virtual-world game. I say that as subdirectory and file names come after the domain name suffix, they are part of the web page's address – and so they are part of the communications of the publishing organization. And as communications is part of marketing, getting the full URL *right* is important.

DOMAIN NAMES IN PRACTICE
The low down on subs

In the same way that second and third level domains are called subdomains, so any directories and files that come after the suffix of a domain name are referred to as subfolders.

The first point is to make the navigation of the site obvious – in web development this is called usability. Take this URL, for example:

www.alancharlesworth.eu/interesting–articles/branding.html. It's hardly rocket science to work out what the content of that page is about. Perhaps more importantly, in an e–commerce environment:

www.atrustingbusiness.com/men/shirts/casual/polo.html tells the user what page they are on or if it is a link, going to. OK, so what? You might ask, and it might not make a big difference in the great scheme of things – but some things are just *better* if they are done *right*. But wait, I have another argument up my sleeve which goes beyond the intangible concept of *looking right*. As we saw in the previous section, search engines like to find keywords in domain names – and supporters of that notion say that it also applies to the full URL. Only the engineers at Google, Yahoo!, Bing et al can say if I am right, but surely a search engine would look at:

www.atrustingbusiness.com/men/shirts/polo.html and think that something on that page *should* match the needs of a searcher who types "men's polo shirt" into the search box? Secondly, if you are going to match web page URLs with their content, stick to characters that make sense. I would argue that you should use only those characters that are allowed in a domain name – and this includes the 'no–spaces' rule (a space in a URL can show in browser navigation bars as '%20'). Within the directories and files, I would use hyphens to distinguish the words rather than 'all-one-word', eg 'interesting–articles' rather than 'interestingarticles' in my earlier example. Avoiding upper-case letters is also a good idea. It's not a big issue if the URL is a link, but as far as computer files are concerned 'InterestingArticles' is a different file name to 'interestingarticles' (try it with your own word documents). Depending on your PC's operating system – or that of your site's host – the URL may or may not be case sensitive, so I say; don't take the chance, put them all in lower case. And finally, don't use the underscore (_) in anything related to the Internet. The simple reason for this is that when a link appears on a web page, the default setting is for that to be in bold, blue and underlined – and if a file name with an underscore is underlined, the underscore looks like a space (eg interesting_articles is presented as <u>interesting articles</u>).

DOMAIN NAMES IN PRACTICE
a sound investment

In June 2006 investment advisers Facility International ran ads in the print media promoting the international element of their investment portfolio. In the ads they featured the URL www.fidelity.co.uk/intl.

I say, why '/intl' and not '/international'? Not only is 'intl' *not* the normal abbreviation of international (it's 'int'), but the promotion is about *international* investment, it's not a hard word to spell – why confuse the issue with this abbreviation. Wouldn't www.fidelity.co.uk/international have been a better choice?

Having criticised their URL construction, however, fidelity.co.uk is a good example of registering the domain of the name by which a company is commonly known (more of this in chapter 3.04). The actual trading name of the company is Fidelity International, and the small print in the ad also mentions Fidelity *Investment Funds*, Fidelity *Unit Trusts* and Fidelity *Investment Services* Ltd. All this adds up to make the generic fidelity.co.uk an ideal domain name for this group of companies.

1.14   WHAT DO YOU NEED TO DO IF YOU ARE CHANGING YOUR DOMAIN NAME?

In answer to the question raised in the title of this section, I would suggest that such is the upheaval concerned, are you really, really sure you have to change your domain name? Changing your domain just for the sake of change – like changing the shade of background colour on your corporate logo, for example – is not a good idea. Of course, it could be that you *have* to change your domain – perhaps you've:

1. Lost your domain name because you failed to renew it

2. Lost your domain name because you were not the registered owner (see chapter 1.01)

3. Changed your trading name

4. Merged with, or have been taken over by, another company

Even at this stage, I would still ask if there is any other solution to changing your domain name. If, however, there is no other option, points three and four are nothing like as challenging as the first two.

The reason for this is that if you are moving to a new domain *voluntarily* you still have control over the original name. This means that you can redirect visitors to your new domain, and so all existing customers who have bookmarked your site or have any literature with the old domain name will find themselves on your new site without realizing it – though you might want to put a message on the new site letting folk know the site has changed domains. With regard to search engine optimization, it is important to use a '301' status code (which means the site has moved *permanently*) so that the search engines recognize this and 'transfer' any search status your old pages may have accrued over the years (for more on the practice of redirecting, see the *domain names in practice* in chapter 1.11).

If you have lost your domain name (ie someone else has it), then this is so problematic that I would suggest biting the bullet and paying the asking price (from whomever) and buy it back. As you will have already learned in chapter 1.09, there are folks out there who will happily take any traffic that is visiting your 'old' domain, whether it be for a shopping comparison site or worse still, a competitor. If you cannot recover your domain, you must make all of your existing customers aware of your new domain name. This is a significant, inconvenient – and not least, expensive – undertaking, but it is possible. What may be impossible, however, is reaching all those *potential* customers whose names and contact details you do not know. That is, everyone you ever gave a business card to and everyone who has picked up a piece of your promotional literature since you went online. All of this will need to be replaced. For a full list of what will need to be changed to the new domain, see chapter 4.01 about flaunting your domain name – and you can add company transport and product packaging as a cost that might match stationery.

If you have *chosen* to change your domain – a re-branding exercise, perhaps – all of these *offline* changes will simply be part of the wider logistic issue of changing *all* company logos, merchandise and so on. Expensive it may be, but at least it can be planned and budgeted for.

But wait, that's not all – there is even worse news. If an existing customer types your old domain name into their browser and gets a price comparison site (or worse) instead of yours they may well simply type your company name into a search engine – and so they *should* find your new site (though you might want to consider buying SERP ads for a while if your site has lost some search 'juice' because of the move).

No, what is worse is that your domain name is not just the home of your website, it is your email address. So if that old customer sends an email to the address they used for a previous purchase they will get a bounced email back saying it cannot be delivered. They *might* go online and search for your company website and find the [new] email address on there – but you might not be the only supplier they emailed – and the others have already responded to that communication. Is your product really so good that the customer will take time out to find you when a competitor's email is sitting in their inbox? And what about all those suppliers and other contacts that have your old email address – particularly those who won't be bothered to find you? It would be a shame for your factory to be closed down because you have not responded to an email from the local Health and Safety office. Or your insurance policy lapse because the renewal-notice email never reached you.

Like your website, if you still have control of your 'old' domain name you can arrange email forwarding – but as I said at the beginning of this section, if you can avoid changing your domain name – please do so.

A caveat to all of this, however, is one which is inherent in many sections of this book. That is: it all depends on your commitment or dependence on the Internet in the way you go about your business. For the global entity that is re-branding to a new (brand) name then changing your domain name is a key undertaking. For the local hairdresser's shop that has a one-page website (with little more than opening times on it) and which does not feature high in the search engine index, changing their domain is unlikely to even be noticed by the majority of customers – though it still should be done properly!

CHAPTER 2

the legal aspects of

domain names

Important note

I do not profess to be a legal expert. For full and accurate information on specific details of legal issues with regard to domain names you should contact a qualified lawyer/attorney. For this reason I've kept this chapter short – effectively pointing out those topics about which you should seek qualified legal advice.

2.01 DOMAIN NAMES YOU SHOULD NOT REGISTER

Before registering any domain name for your business and/or organization you should perform due diligence on that name to check that it is not a registered trademark, patent or recognized brand. Of course, you might argue that 'owners' of such names should have already registered the relevant domain names – but perhaps they have registered only their country TLD and you are in a different region. What you don't want is a court case several years down the line when that organization diversifies into your country (or they finally get round to enforcing their trademark), and you have to change the domain name on a site for which you have spent years developing its online brand – that is, its domain name.

In most cases a simple Google search on the term will be sufficient – but if big money is concerned, having qualified folk check the relevant legal registrations (eg patents) is advisable. And don't forget new trademarks are registered every day, so if you come up with a 'unique' domain name it will be worthwhile taking the necessary steps to secure it for the future.

DOMAIN NAMES IN PRACTICE

calling the wrong [i]tune

In 2000 the domain name itunes.co.uk was registered by CyberBritain Holdings. This was some three years before Apple registered the itunes.com domain name and launched iTunes in the States (the UK campaign following a year later), but only a month before the iTunes trademark was registered. Early in 2005, Nominet responded to Apple's complaint and ruled that the name be transferred to Apple.

It would seem that Nominet considered that the registering of the name was more than a lucky guess – though CyberBritian's offer to sell the domain to Napster, a competitor of Apple's iTunes service, and also that for a short time redirecting itunes.co.uk to (iTunes' competitor) napster.co.uk would seem to have had some bearing in the decision.

2.02 HOW ARE DOMAIN NAME

DISPUTES RESOLVED?

Disputes occur when recognized trading or brand names are registered by parties other than the owners of those names. Despite being slow off the mark, most countries have now addressed the issue within their legal systems. For example, in the USA the Anti-cybersquatting Consumer Protection Act of 1999 (ACPA) allows trademark holders to sue for possession of Internet addresses that are the same or 'confusingly similar' to their trademarked names. The somewhat self-describing Truth in Domain Names Act (part the PROTECT Act 2003) aims to prevent the exploitation of children. Although there are now similar laws in the EU, early cases relied on the application of existing laws that pertained to the *use* of a domain name rather than the actual registering of it – and those cases are now part of the legal system.

Originally, the registering authorities washed their hands of the legal issues, though subsequently the Internet Corporation for Assigned Names and Numbers (ICANN) has introduced an arbitration system for resolving disputes. In this, disputing parties each make their case to an independent panel of arbitration that is overseen by accredited organizations such as the World Intellectual Property Organization (WIPO).

In the UK, Nominet UK, the Oxford-based Registry for .uk domain names, has a dispute resolution procedure which has been in force since September 2001. Under Nominet UK's arbitration procedure, the complaining party must assert that It has rights in respect of a name or mark which is identical or similar to the domain name and that the domain name is an abusive registration. The arbitration system is much quicker than normal court proceedings for trade mark infringement – and considerably cheaper.

However, decisions made by both ICANN and Nominet are not binding in the courts, meaning that if a complaining party is unsuccessful in arbitration it can still pursue the domain name registrant through the courts. This lack of legal standing stems from these domain name dispute resolution policies being, essentially, in place to deal with cybersquatters – and are not a substitute for trade mark infringement proceedings.

As new domains become available, their creation has been supported by well thought-out dispute-resolution procedures. The .me.uk names are a good example, applying their Eligibility Requirements Dispute Resolution Policy (ERDRP) – a version of the Uniform Domain Name Dispute Resolution Policy (UDRP) adapted for .name domains. The ERDRP rules state that any complainant must prove all of the following three points:

1. The name corresponding to the registered name is not the legal name of respondent (the owner)

2. The name corresponding to the registered name is not the name of a fictional character in which the respondent has trademark or service mark rights

3. The respondent has not been commonly known by the name corresponding with the registered name.

In addition, the complainant must also fulfil similar criteria themselves, showing at least one of the following:

1. The registered name should be the same as the legal name of complainant, or

2. The registered name is the name of a fictional character in which complainant has trademark or service mark rights, or

3. The Complainant has been commonly known by the registered name.

The principles embedded within the ERDRP make it much easier for rightful owners – celebrities in particular – to recover .name domains. This contrasts with other procedures, such as the UDRP, which has seen personalities such as Sting and even the late Albert Einstein losing domain disputes. Whilst these rules apply only to the .name domains (and so are, by definition, names of individuals), it is not difficult to see how they might be adopted for brand, company or product names.

A brief examination of a few of the significant cases in domain name disputes that have made it to the courts will give you some idea of how future disputes are likely to be resolved. The first two are from the UK and are important in that as they were the first such cases they became *case law* referred to by other countries.

- **Pitman Training Limited vs Pearson Professional Ltd (t/a Pitman Publishing)** The first UK court ruling on a domain name issue, this is essentially a case of two companies who both trade under the same name –

Pitman – each claiming the right to use a domain name. There is a sub plot to this in that one party registered the name first but did not use it, and the other 'claimed' it from the registering authority. The judge found that whenever two parties have equal claim to a domain name, then whoever registers it first becomes the rightful owner – the so called 'first come, first served' rule that has been universally applied since.

- **Harrods and others** In this case high-end retailer Harrods brought the lawsuit, although there were a number of other parties who had been 'wronged' by the defendant. The defendant registered a number of domains in the names of household-name companies and then offered to sell the names to those organizations. The judge found that the registration of a domain name that is the trademark of another was not an offence in itself. However, an offence was committed as the defendant 'clearly constituted infringement of Harrods' registered trade marks and passing off'. It is arguable, therefore, that had the defendant simply waited for the companies to contact him with an offer of purchase rather than contacting them then he would have committed no offence.

Cases from outside the UK that have had an impact on domain name related laws include:

- **Sex.com** A protracted case that has a plot of which John Grisham would be proud (the book and the film can't be far away). The name was originally registered by [then] student Gary Kremen. He did nothing with the name. The villain of this piece, Stephen Cohen, then forged a transfer document that the registering authority (Network Solutions) rather naively accepted as real. Mr Cohen, an experienced operator in the pornography industry, went on to build a significant business around the domain name. Mr Kremen did not realise he had 'lost' the name until Mr Cohen had been using the name for some time. Kremen then commenced legal proceedings against not only the pornographer but Network Solutions for the negligence in the transfer. The case ran for a number of years, but ultimately the judge declared Mr Kremen to be the legitimate owner. The importance of this decision was in not only establishing the legal precedent that Internet domains were legal property, but the ruling of how much the guilty party had gained through its use – effectively putting a value on potential commercial applications of a domain name. In this case the judge decided that the pornographer owed Mr Kremen $65 million. The story doesn't end there however, as Mr Cohen fled the country and has yet to pay anything. Network Solutions did not get off scot-free. Kremen also sued them and was paid around $15 million to settle the lawsuit in April 2004 (note that the payment was made by VeriSign, who had inherited the case when it acquired Network Solutions). In January of 2006, Kremen sold the name for a sum reported to be anything from 12 to 14 million dollars – though that sum also included the business based on the domain, and not just the domain name itself.

- **Nissan.com** – Another story with a number of twists, this is a classic David versus Goliath story. It all started with a North Carolina businessman called Uri Nissan who, in the early days of the world wide web, registered nissan.com for the website of his computer-related products and services business. When the global car manufacturer realised that the web was to become an integral part of car sales they wheeled out the big (and expensive) legal guns and took Mr Nissan to court. Mr Nissan used the web to gain support for his cause and eventually won the case. The judge ruled that as Mr Nissan's nissan.com website was clearly about computer-related products [and not cars] he was not misusing the domain (his website's front page even included a link to the Nissan Motors website for those who found themselves there by mistake) – and he registered it first! Subsequently, however, Mr Nissan allowed the car giant's lawyers another day in court by selling advertising space on nissan.com's front page to other car manufacturers. Although Mr Nissan won this battle, the ware, it seems, is not over. A message from Mr Nissan on nissan.com says:

'Nissan Motor is attempting to obtain a Federal Trademark Registration for computers and computer peripherals among other classes of goods and services. We feel that Nissan Motor, in this action, is staging a future case against us in the computer and peripherals market.'

Mr Nissan suggests that Nissan Motors' legal fees for this case currently stand at around three million dollars. I bet Nissan's management wish that back in 1999 they had simply made Uri a financial offer he couldn't refuse instead of taking legal action. If nothing else, Nissan.com would be helping to sell cars and not damaging their reputation every time someone goes to it.

- **Student prank** For those offended by swearing, skip this paragraph. In this story, once again, car manufacturers are involved – this time in a domain name spoof perpetrated as a joke by a group of American students. They registered the domain fuckgeneralmotors.com (don't ask how it got past the '7 filthy words' rule) and made it live, but actually redirected surfers to ford.com. The students were taken to court not by General Motors, but Ford – who claimed that people might think it was they (Ford) who had perpetrated the prank. The judge declared that it was obviously a spoof and dismissed the case, but the domain name was withdrawn by ICANN anyway.

- **Big hammer to crack a small nut** – in late 2003, Vancouver teenager Mike Rowe received an email from Smart & Biggar, Microsoft's Canadian lawyers (yes, that really is their name) informing him that he had been committing copyright infringement against Microsoft. His crime? Because his part-time business sold software, he added 'soft' to his own name and registered the domain name – mikerowesoft.com.
  In a subsequent email Microsoft offered Mike $10 for the domain name, which he found 'insulting' and replied explaining how much work he had put into the

business and that the domain was worth at least $10000. And therein lays Mike's big mistake, he fell for the standard trap set by large corporations in small-fry domain disputes. The mega-corp offers a few dollars for the registration fee, and so goads the domain owner into a counter-offer. The mere fact that a counter–offer is made is taken – in the convoluted arbitration process – as prima facia evidence that the owner is a cybersquatter who is attempting to extort cash. Result: big company wins domain name.

And of course we would all have got mikerowesoft.com and microsoft.com mixed up wouldn't we?

Postscript; because of the publicity that this story generated (Mike was interviewed on, amongst others, CNN) Microsoft subsequently backed down, a spokesman saying, 'We take our trademark seriously, but in this case maybe a little too seriously' The name was eventually exchanged for, amongst other things, an Xbox console.

More recently, as the web has become accepted as an integral element of both business and marketing, disputes where a brand or trade name are only *part* of a domain name have become common. Two examples involving .coms are these:

- **Volvospares.com** This ruling went against Swedish car maker Volvo who had complained about a website trading under this domain. The decision being that although the domain name was 'confusingly similar' to Volvo's trade mark, the domain's owners had a legitimate business interest in using the name.

- **Raleighbikes.com** The owners of the Raleigh trade mark argued this was a clear infringement of their intellectual property rights, but again ICANN disagreed, ruling in favour of raleighbikes.com because its owner was using the name for a non-commercial forum site for fans of Raleigh bikes and had not registered the name in bad faith. In marketing terms, Raleigh committed a significant gaffe in this example – suing some of your most vociferous supporters (read customers) is not something you will find in the manual of good public relations practice.

I conclude this chapter with a repeat of my comments at its start.

I am not a lawyer. This chapter is not legal advice. Do not rely on any of it to support any legal argument. If any of the content seems relevant to your situation, go find someone who has the legal qualifications to comment on your case.

CHAPTER 3

domain name choice:

getting it *right*

Whilst I can appreciate that many readers will have skipped the previous pages to get to this chapter because it is 'what you bought the book for', the first two chapters WILL help you choose the *right* domain name, so read them before this chapter – it will save you time in the end!

3.01 CHOOSING THE *RIGHT* SUFFIX

In general, the content of this book is equally pertinent to organizations all around the world. However, such is the nature of the domain name system that the United States stands alone in the subject of suffixes. Effectively, the rest of the world has more choice than America. (I mentioned it earlier in the book, but don't forget that in the USA a domain name's *suffix* is also commonly referred to as the *extension*). This is because US suffixes are not only *available*, but also *useful*, to organizations globally. Whilst domain names of some other countries are available to American companies – and in limited instances, beneficial – it is rare for a US organization to even consider registering a non-US-regulated domain.

However, for readers in the United States to skip this section would be a mistake. Not only are uses of the various US-administered (eg .info) and non-country specific domains (eg .cc) addressed, but the decision-making process for an American business considering the use of a .us suffix mirrors that of an organization from elsewhere deciding on whether to register a .com or use their own country's suffix.

The essential issues to be addressed are (a) the nature of the organization, and (b) where it trades now or may do in the future. If the organization is a commercial entity – business – then the main choice is between the local suffix and .com.

Using a UK company and the .co.uk suffix as an example, if the business trades only in the UK then .co.uk is the suffix to choose. If the business trades globally, then .com is the better option. This is, of course, rather simplistic. So what are options in the grey areas that sit between the black and white? Considerations for that UK company include:

- If the business wants to be *perceived* as being a global player (even if it isn't), then perhaps .com is better

- If the business wants to be perceived as being a global player, but wants to be identified as being from the UK (perhaps the product or service benefits from the association), then .co.uk is better

- If the business trades in Europe – rather than globally – then .co.uk is generally better

- If not to be immediately identified as being from the UK is preferred, go for .com

- Where promotion might be global but the location of the product is critical. Hotels are an obvious example – nicehotel.com, for instance, could be anywhere in the world, whereas nicehotel.co.uk is obviously (somewhere) in the UK.

For American readers, these examples could just as easily be a business in any state in the US. A company in Dallas, for example, who only trades in that city or state, might consider a .tx.us domain as an alternative to a .com (note that authorities in Texas – and other states – also use third level domains on the suffix, for example .lib.tx.us for libraries).

In a wider context it could be that the product's unique selling proposition is that it originates from a distinct region – in which case that region's suffix is preferable. Isklar Water, which markets itself as being made from Norwegian Glaciers, sensibly uses isklar.no, for example. Similarly, a US company might use a 'state'.us domain for the same reason.

Gaining popularity outside the US are the regional options of .eu and .asia – with other regions set to join these in the future (.uae for the United Arab Emirates, for example). As with the .co.uk examples above, these suffixes can be used to identify organizations from specific locations – but without being country-specific. Perhaps an attraction of these suffixes – so my international students and business contacts tell me – is that they are *not* .com. That is, *not* American. Whether it is a result of US foreign policy or regional pride – or somewhere in between – many folk around the globe see the .com as an association with America, and so would prefer to avoid the suffix but at the same time prefer a 'global' suffix to that of their own country.

Although it is becoming more popular in the US, where there are more businesses chasing what names there are, using a *novelty* suffix when the *best* one (ie, the .com) has gone can be an option. However, any company that registers a .cc, .tv or .ws name should do so with caution. There is a perception that a company with a *novelty* domain is not a *reputable* business.

DOMAIN NAMES IN PRACTICE

do as I say, not as I do

I could argue that my website sits on a .eu domain because I reside in Europe and I'm a member of the expanding European community. Although I am quite happy to have my site on alancharlesworth.eu, would I prefer it to be on alancharlesworth.com or alancharlesworth.co.uk? Yes, I probably would – and I'm not because despite my working in 'e-commerce' since 1996, I never envisaged a time when I would want a website of my own, on my own domain. So I never bothered to register my own name as 'all-one-word'.

Doh!

A further problem with novelty domains is that you might want to check what kind of company hosts a website on the .com equivalent in case there is either conflict or embarrassment. It is likely that a surfer – particularly in the USA – will assume that the .com is the domain name of any company they might come across. Therefore, if your company is called A Trusting Business, customers are likely go to atrustingbusiness.com expecting the website of your business (which is actually on atrustingbusiness.biz) but instead of your products they might find ladies' lingerie. That might be simply embarrassing, but it would be even worse if the site had pornographic content! There is also the possibility that the .com website sells products similar to yours – not such a far-fetched notion if generic words have been used in the primary name – and the customer buys from that company instead of yours. For example, are dolls.com, dolls.co.uk, dolls.eu, dolls.biz and dolls.cc the websites for the same or different purveyors of toys, or do they host sites with pornographic content? (At the time of writing they are four domainer sites and a domain for sale – which is interesting, see chapter 1.08 on generic-word domains and 1.09 on domains that generate income). Note that it is for this reason that in the section on registering domain names for a global organization (chapter 1.11) I suggest registering multiple suffixes of the chosen name.

However, there might be instances where a suffix away from the accepted business norm can be effective. Although I would never advise a pure-play online-only business to take this route, it can work for offline organizations where the web is for marketing support rather than being essential for sales or lead generation. For example, a .net where the inference is that the domain name is the organization 'on the net' might work for a club or society. Similarly, .info could be used for a website that provides technical support for a product supplied exclusively offline – farm machinery, perhaps, or specific safety data for chemicals. Note that the .org should be left to not-for-profit organizations. In my opinion, having a company trading on a .org is bad practice – and may even be perceived by users as a commercial firm masquerading as a charity.

Whilst a .biz domain might be considered a poor second choice after .com, there are other suffixes – introduced around the same time as .biz – that carry some validity, not least because their use is restricted. In particular .jobs, .travel,

.museum and .aero can only be registered by organizations in those industries. However, as all companies that existed at the time of the introduction of these names had already created emails addresses and online presences on .com domains, these remain largely unused – even by new entities. Indeed, such is the scarcity of these names that on the rare occasions I come across them I have to look twice to appreciate them. The Egyptian Tourist Authority, for example, frequently advertises in UK newspapers using the domain name Egypt.travel – and every time I see it my first thought is that a misprint has omitted the suffix from a third level domain (ie egypt.travel.com). Given that this confuses someone who has written a book on domain names, I would suggest less experienced web-users might be puzzled also. Having said this, of course, as time goes on – and demand for domains increases – perhaps these new suffixes (the .pro included) might become the '.coms' for the next generation of Internet users.

DOMAIN NAMES IN PRACTICE
no credit for this choice of name

Personal loans company *One Call* use the domain name onecall.ws. I had to look up for which country ws is the suffix (it's Western Semao). Sorry One Call, because the ws carries no credibility at all, I'd have taken a different route. In the context of loans it might even give the perception of being some kind of 'offshore' operation.

At the time I first saw a TV ad for One Call that included the onecall.ws domain the following were available: onecall.tv, onecall.info, onecall–loans and onecallonline on a variety of suffixes (though not .com and .co.uk) – and onecall–online were available for every common suffix.

Beyond the accepted norms (.com etc) and the newcomers (.jobs etc) come what I have previously described as 'novelty' suffixes. Most of these are just that – novelties, and are not really options for the majority of organizations. I would always advise that second, third, fourth or even fifth choice names on reputable suffixes are preferable to 'good' names based on *novelty* suffixes. Some of these, however, might have limited applications. One, .cc (from the Cocos Islands) for example, might be linked to motorcycles – they are identified by the cubic capacity (cc) of their engines, eg 250cc. Another is the .tv suffix (from Tuvalu) which can be associated with any company in the television industry – or in TV advertising. Financial services is an industry that has benefited greatly from the web as a medium for promotion, therefore mortgages.com is a very valuable name – and it was registered early on in the domain name 'gold rush'. A reasonable alternative, for use purely on TV adverts for a finance company, is mortgages.tv. This domain name has been registered by APS Mortgages (UK) Ltd who used it in a television advertising campaign.

A further use of some of the more unusual suffixes is to make up so called 'domain hacks' where the suffix becomes part of a product, brand or organization's name. These are rare and normally used by non-commercial entities where the novelty element is not an impediment. For example, a nice use of .net comes from the UK's Higher Education Funding Councils' education and research network, JANET – it uses ja.net. Whilst two character names are hard to get (read, virtually impossible), any organization that has a name ending in *net* – or any other suffix, org for example – might consider this route.

Another example is blo.gs (gs is the TLD for South Georgia and the South Sandwich Islands), but my favourite use of a name and suffix to make a word is the social bookmarking website – del.icio.us – a third level name based on icio.us. If you happen to be in North America, then perhaps the .us can be practical if used with a verb that describes what you want a customer to do – contact.us or join.us, perhaps. Note that I picked these two verbs at random – such is the way of things in the crazy world of domain names that the first is the domain of Contact Labelling Systems, whilst join.us takes surfers to the website of the Scheiner Law Group – go figure.

DOMAIN NAMES IN PRACTICE
when 'it' ain't what it should be

Featured in a UK newspaper was an ad for the Piemonte region of Italy – with a tagline of 'Piemonte, feel it'. As the Italian suffix is .it, the domain name used for the promotion was piemontefeel.it. I suppose it must have looked good in the pitch, and I am all for inventive uses of suffixes, but this just didn't work. I had to look twice before I realized what was going on – and I'm *supposed* to be an *expert*.

3.02 CHOOSING THE *RIGHT* DOMAIN NAME – GENERAL ADVICE

In subsequent sections we will look at creating domain names for specific purposes, each having different criteria for the selection process. There are, however, some principles that are generic to all purposes – though their proposed application will be the ultimate decider. These basic principles include:

- Length – in general, when picking a name, less is more. However, as you will see later in this chapter, this is not an absolute. If a long domain name is the *right* domain name for its purpose, then that is the one you should register.

- How easy is it to recall the name? If you expect customers to remember your domain name, then it must be easy to recollect. In some instances this is where short or generic domains can be best. On the other hand, if you knew my company name was Charlesworth that's what you would remember – all 12 letters of it. For me to have a website on 'charles' because it is shorter would only confuse the issue.

- How will it be communicated? The medium – or media – in which customers will engage with your domain name will influence your choice. Considerations include:

    o   Radio (verbal only) – particularly relevant for radio *advertising*, there cannot be any confusion in what is being said. Vocally, 'two', 'to', 'too' and '2' all sound the same, but as part of a domain name each is different

    o   Print media (visual) – this is where short and

memorable can be moved down the list of essential criteria because users will be able type the domain into a browser whilst reading it from print

- TV and outside advertising (brief visual) – not only are short and memorable important, but being aesthetically clear and easy to read also come into the equation

- Telephone (verbal only) – similar to radio, but add in the potential for distortion and the speaker's accent or pronunciation

- Word of mouth (verbal) – in this case the context can be important. Teenagers, for example, might expect 'for' to be '4'

All of these issues are addressed in the following sections, but here's one example to get things started.

MACH3Turbo.com is the domain name used by Gillette (a Procter and Gamble company) in the advertising for their men's razor of the same name. The interesting thing here is that Gillette actually present the domain name as I have here, with the same use of upper case letters as they use on the packaging of the product, ie 'MACH 3 Turbo' is the brand logo. Whilst this practice should be applauded, there is a caveat to the use of numbers in a domain name. If Gillette ran an advert for the razor on the radio and the voiceover made the comment 'for more details go to our website on mach three turbo dot com' – what would you type into your browser, 3 or three? I checked. Gillette hasn't registered machthreeturbo.com. I think the company could have stretched their marketing budget to a cover an extra name, don't you? There is a further lesson to be taken from this example. If a domain name is to be communicated only verbally, consider the way the recipient would spell what they heard. If I heard the phrase 'mach three' I would immediately associate it with speed through the air and spell it accordingly (as it is in this product). In a less than scientific experiment I asked my wife and her sister to write down 'mach three'. One wrote 'mac 3' and the other 'mack three'. I would accept the argument that the MACH 3 Turbo is a men's razor, and so they *might* be more likely to associate 'mach' with speed, but it is a thin argument.

Another product that uses a number in its name is Wall's Magnum Seven Sins ice cream, which uses magnum7sins.com as its domain name. However, Wall's recognized the numbers issue and registered magnumsevensins.com as well – well done them.

DOMAIN NAMES IN PRACTICE

the Internet is global

Your website can be seen around the world, which means your domain name will be read by folk of various nationalities whose first language is not that in which the name is presented – so beware of word combinations being lost in pronunciation. For example, UK energy provider Powergen (now re–branded as Eon) found itself fielding embarrassing questions about their Italian division's website's domain name – powergenitalia.com. What made this so frustrating for them was that Powergen had no Italian division – the name belongs to an Italian battery firm that was unaware that running the two elements of its name together in its domain name would prove amusing to English speakers. Not really that big of a deal, but in a global market it is worth checking.

3.03 ARE GENERIC WORDS EFFECTIVE AS DOMAIN NAMES?

The answer to the question raised in the title of this section is yes. And no.

If you are looking to develop a business model around domain names, then generic names will make money (see chapter 1.09). Similarly, if you are starting a new online venture which has no established brand, then developing that brand around a generic term can work. It is also the case that generic domains can be used to generate visitor numbers to an existing business. Indeed, some of the highest priced domain name sales fall in this category – loans.com, for example (more on *why* later). However, for the existing or new, *offline* business looking to develop the role of the Internet in its marketing, a generic domain is far from ideal – and given that they cost a lot to purchase, not really a viable option.

DOMAIN NAMES IN PRACTICE
generic terms are not always an option

Whilst many – if not most – countries allow generic words to be created on their TLD suffixes, this is not absolute. Some countries block generic words (including town and city names) in order to prevent the type of problems that have arisen over their ownership or to prevent the names becoming saleable commodities. Other registries insist that only the names of recognized entities (organizations, companies etc) can be registered.

So why can generic domain names be a good idea? The basis of the argument revolves around the practice of web users typing a domain directly into a browser with the hope that it will host a website whose content matches the domain name. For example, to mend a leaking tap, I might type in 'plumber.com'. It has to be said, however, that this practice is far more common in the USA that it is elsewhere in the world – the dominance of the .com being the reason. It is for this reason that generic names are so popular with operators of the quazi-shopping comparison sites that can make their owners a lot of money (see chapter 1.08).

However, the same principle applies to those legitimate website developers who look to provide a service whereby information on a specific subject is compiled in such a way as it is a benefit to users. Popular with the travel industry – tripadvisor.com is a good example – these sites also have a business model of earning income from clickthroughs on ads, but at least the visitor gains some benefit from the content of the site, the publishers having put some effort into developing that content.

Generic names can also work if an organization is inextricably linked by consumers with a product or service – something that is normally the result of brand building which pre-dates their move onto the Internet. These are in the minority however, with good examples being few and far between. In this category I would include fruits.com - the domain name of del Monte (in this case, the domain name man, he say 'yes') and UK do-it-yourself retail giant, B&Q whose site can be found on diy.com (diy.co.uk also redirects to diy.com).

Other examples of generic domains that are used by purveyors of the 'named' products include: books.com (Barnes & Noble), pc.com (Intel), loans.com (Bank of America), rentalcar.com (Enterprise) and paper.co.uk (Premier Paper Group). Note that in instances such as these I would advise the organizations to host corporate information on the 'company' domain name and use the generic domains for marketing activities.

One effective application of having the domain name of the product is where the business operates only online, with the domain name being not only the name of the company but so also the brand. A good example of this is the hotel search and comparison site, hotel.com. The company I worked with back in the day – and where I learned most of this domain name stuff up in the front line – is another example. It was called domainnames.com. You can see how I had an edge when I was pitching for domain name registration business.

DOMAIN NAMES IN PRACTICE

cleaning up generic names

In the early days of the commercial web, consumer products giant Procter and Gamble registered a whole host of generic words that might be connected to their product ranges, including cavities.com, disinfect.com, soap.com, cleans.com, dry.com, flu.com, nails.com, scent.com, thirst.com and towels.com. As few of the names have been used on websites P&G's original motives are not clear – presumably to use on information-type websites or simply redirect them to the brand sites. Whatever their initial plans, the multi-national giant has abandoned them, announcing in July 2006 that they intended to sell many of the generic domain names registered in the previous decade.

However, any generic-domain strategy comes with inherent problems. As with the majority of online marketing, the lessons are in traditional marketing – learned over centuries of offline trading. The key problem is that a generic name promotes a *category* rather than a *company*. In the offline world few companies use generic words or phrases as a brand. For example, in the UK we have Tesco, the USA Walmart and mainland Europe Carrefore, but nowhere has 'Grocery Store'. This is the case because each company wants to develop a distinct brand identity – so differentiating it against competitors. Although a descriptive name can bring recognition in the early days of the new online business, in the long term it is can be counter productive.

Take Amazon for example. Had the original name been amazonbooks.com, the company that was to become one of the first big online brands would have had difficulty expanding to the various products and services it now offers. In the early days of the Internet, companies perceived that naming the company as a generic domain name would have advantages – a perception that has logical foundations. In the offline world, customers have numerous contextual clues to identify the company or brand. The shape of a bottle will tell you it is Coke. The fast food restaurant with the Golden Arches is McDonalds. In the virtual world, however, these contextual clues do not exist. Furthermore, the online customer searches by product or service category. A new web surfer looking for online groceries, for example, might be attracted to eGrocer rather than webvan – the latter sounding more like a website that sells vehicles. That might have been the case some years ago, but now any new surfer's search return is likely to also include the website of a brand they recognize, so curtailing the need for the domain name that matches the product category.

The dot com boom and bust is littered with generic names that failed in the same industry or market as 'proper' names that succeeded. For example:

successful proper names	Generic domains that didn't make it
Yahoo	searchengine.com
Monster	jobs.com
Expedia	travel.com
eBay	auction.com
Amazon	books.com (Barnes & Noble bought the domain when the original business failed)

So, with regard to generic-word domain names being effective there is no real answer – though if you want to make any money from domain names as the foundation of a business model, generic would be the way to go. As for buying one for your new – or existing – business, do your calculations to be sure there will be a return on any investment. It could well be that the money you pay for a suitable generic name might be better spent on promoting a lesser (but still good!) name. (See also chapter 1.12 the role of generic domain names in search engine algorithms).

DOMAIN NAMES IN PRACTICE

retailer couldn't *see* this good domain

I remember approaching one of the UK's leading retail opticians about their purchasing *optician.com* from the organization I represented at the time. I got a terse reply – from their IT dept – saying that they were 'not interested in *novelty* domain names'. Perhaps they were right, but I wonder how much that organization has spent on online advertising since 1997? I do not know what that figure is, but I do know how much they could have bought that prime domain name for – and it was a lot less than a single ad in a single national newspaper on a single day.

I note that optician.com is now a *domaining* site – so someone agrees with me on this one!

3.04 CHOOSING THE *RIGHT* DOMAIN NAME

FOR AN EXISTING ORGANIZATION

Before I start this section, let me say that I do appreciate that company names and trading names might not be the same – Alan Charlesworth Ltd *trading as* Wonder Products, for example. In such cases this chapter will consider only the trading name – in this example, Wonder Products. It is also the case that some elements of this section will apply equally to the next one which looks at choosing domain names for *new* companies.

For both existing and new organizations, the decision on the domain name that will represent it on the Internet will be largely influenced by the online objectives of that organization. For the small business that trades successfully in its local area through offline marketing, a website might add little to that marketing effort – and so the domain name is not *that* important. Don't get me wrong, it is still important to make the *right* decision – but spending thousands of pounds to buy in a generic-term domain is not really a viable option in this scenario. Neither is the decision on using a hyphen because the all-one-word version has been registered going to be something that keeps the owner awake at night. At the opposite end of the spectrum is the new online-only business. For that organization the domain name *could* be the difference between success and failure.

There are currently more existing businesses that have yet to move online than there are new businesses (apparently, around 80% of US small businesses still have no web presence), so this section will probably be the most read in the book. However, the guidelines I offer here are equally relevant to the new business – the subject of the next section.

I have always been a proponent of naming a business with a combination of its location or owner and what it does. If this is the case, then the best domain name option is to simply take the company name, and add the suitable suffix. So if our business makes toys in York and is called York Toys Ltd, we simply combine the two words and add a suffix – yorktoys.co.uk. Similarly, Alan's Toys Ltd would use alanstoys.co.uk. A further option is to combine generic terms with places. For example, how many places have a 'station taxis' (cabs) or 'sea view hotel'? Yet few, if any, locations will have more than one business with the same name. So we can have stationtaxismanchester.co.uk, stationcabschicago.com – or for that matter, liverpoolstationtaxis.co.uk or bostonstationcabs.com.[5] Because you have already read the section on suffixes, I don't need to remind you that for all the variations on a theme as described here you can also use any suffix that is feasible.

Another twist on the add-the-location route is to insert the two-character preposition 'of'. This is not unusual for offline company names where the company is named after a person with a common name. For example, a firm owned by Gerald Hallam that is based in Immingham might be called Hallam's of Immingham – so differentiating it from any other firm that trades under the name Hallam's. If the *offline* name is Hallam's of Immingham then the chances of that domain name

[5] The domain name of the biggest taxi firm in my home city of Sunderland is stationtaxis.com. I wonder who advised them to register such a good generic domain back around 1997? OK, it was me.

being already registered is minimal. But if they did trade simply as Hallam's they have long since missed out on that domain name (all popular suffixes based on hallam and hallams have been registered), so for their website, hallamsofimmingham.com is an effective option.

DOMAIN NAMES IN PRACTICE

apostrophes

That apostrophes cannot be used in domain names should not be a problem when selecting a name. The reason is twofold; (i) it has become accepted practice to register terms that include an apostrophe as domain names *without* that punctuation mark, and (ii) sadly, few people actually know how to use apostrophes correctly, so their absence in a domain name will not even be noticed by most.

There are occasions when the full name and trade of the business might be simply too long to be acceptable as a domain name (realistically, anything over twenty characters is *questionable*). A fabrication welding company from Sunderland, for example, should think seriously before registering sunderlandfabricationwelding.co.uk. Similarly, a refrigeration engineering business in Philadelphia might consider philadelphiarefrigerationengineering.com somewhat unwieldy.

So what to do? One option would be to register a name – nickname – by which the company is commonly known. Organizations with long names are frequently given shorter, more convenient, titles. Such names can be official (the initial letters of the company name, perhaps) or a colloquial abbreviation (Jag, for Jaguar cars, for example). For my fictional Sunderland Fabrication Welding and Philadelphia Refrigeration Engineering I'd start by going down the obvious route of their initials as a domain name. Sadly few, if any, three or four character domain names are still available. In this case sfw.co.uk has been registered by SF Williams Ltd and pre.com (though unused) has been registered by the Harris Corporation of Florida.

Other possibilities for my made–up companies might come from shortening elements of their names as shown in the following table. Note that in this exercise I am concentrating on the actual name only – all of the following can be used with different suffixes.

Sunderland Fabrication Welding	Philadelphia Refrigeration Engineering
sunderlandfabweld	phillyrefrigerationengineering
sunderland-fab-weld	philly-refrigeration-engineering
sundfabweld	phillyrefrigerationeng
sund-fab-weld	philly-refrigeration-eng
sundfabricationwelding	phillyrefeng
sund-fabrication-welding	philly-ref-eng
sunfabricationwelding	philadelphiarefrigerationeng
sun-fabrication-welding	philadelphia-refrigeration-eng

Note that I picked Philadelphia simply because it was the longest American place name that I could think of (watching 'Cold Case' was probably an influence!). That Philadelphia is commonly, and easily, abbreviated to 'Philly' makes many of the suggestions for the refrigeration company far more acceptable than those where Sunderland is rather unnaturally reduced to 'Sund' or 'Sun' – not something that is common practice offline.

Unfortunately, however, none of this list look *right*. I wish I could be more objective and offer a checklist of points to tick-off in order to get the right name, but there is no such list. It is a subjective call. They are just not *right*. Like the discipline of marketing as a whole, choosing a domain name is part art, part science – this is where the art aspect comes in.

So what would I suggest if the owners of these made-up companies knocked on my door and asked my advice? Perhaps taking the route of a generic phrase, for example:

Sunderland Fabrication Welding	Philadelphia Refrigeration Engineering
fabricationwelding.co.uk	refrigerationengineering.com
fabrication–welding.co.uk	refrigeration–engineering.com

Of these, only the two .co.uk names are still available. Generally speaking, all generic words and useful combinations thereof have already been registered, but there are some combinations still out there, particularly in the more traditional trades that have been relatively late in joining the information superhighway.

However, to have a website sitting on such a generic domain will result in the organization's brand being divided – in marketing terms, a serious error.

Given that the best combinations of 'fabrication welding' and 'refrigeration engineering' are no longer available, what domain names should my two fictitious firms go for?

Well ... remember those two suggestions that I dismissed so lightly at the beginning of this example because they were too long? You will recall I said 'realistically anything over twenty characters is questionable' – and OK, both sunderlandfabricationwelding.co.uk and philadelphiarefrigerationengineering.com might both be rather long, but they are probably the *best* options. Why? you might ask. To which I would argue that in these two examples both of these suggested domain names tell you exactly what the company does and where it is from. For me, the advantages of that trumps the 'over-long' issue.

DOMAIN NAMES IN PRACTICE
less than mobile

The North East Mobility Warehouse has the domain name northeastmob.com. This company is local to me in the North East of England, but they certainly didn't ask me for advice before choosing their domain name. Let's start with the suffix - a .com for a company whose customer base must be in its own locale? The actual name sounds as though it should belong to the website of a group of football hooligans. In Yellow Pages the company is listed as North East Mobility Warehouse. When you ring them, the greeting is 'North East Mobility'. So where does northeastmob.com come from? I can only think that they (or their advisers) thought a shorter name would be better. Superior options? It's a small company, so I don't think multiple registrations are necessary. I would go for northeastmobilitywarehouse.co.uk or if you want a shorter version, and particularly if the company refers to itself without the 'warehouse' – as the phone answer would suggest – northeastmobility.co.uk (at the time of writing, both of these names were available).

3.05 CHOOSING THE *RIGHT* DOMAIN NAME FOR A NEW COMPANY

In many ways this is easier than choosing a domain name for an existing company in that the marketer starts with a blank sheet of paper. As stated in the previous section, the nature of the business will largely determine the importance of the domain name. Needless to say, if the web is to play a significant role in the marketing of my new venture I would look for a company name that has not already been registered as a domain name. For the small to medium firm that trades predominantly offline, the chances are that the 'best' business name will also be the best domain name – and it will be available to register (as in my Hallam's of Immingham example).

In the case of the new venture, there is something of a chicken and egg situation – as in, 'what comes first, the domain name or the company name?' Well, for the offline company that will have a website as an element of its marketing efforts I would go with the best company name and see if the best domain name is available for it. Going back to Mr Hallam in the previous section, let's say he is starting a new haulage business – so we are talking about a name that will be displayed on 40 foot trailers as well as two-inch business cards. In which case he could call his business simply 'Hallam's', 'Hallam's of Immingham' 'Hallam's Transport', ' Hallam's Haulage', 'Hallam's Freight', 'Hallam's Transport of Immingham' ... well, you get my drift. If I were his marketing advisor I would say pick whichever name you like best, and then check to see if the domain name was available. If it wasn't (and that would suggest a business of that name already exists and so would be a problem when registering the company for legal purposes), then go to the second choice company name and check that domain name. Naturally, suffixes will come into the equation. If there is already an American company called Smith's of Washington with the domain name smithsofwashington.com, then a company in Washington, England could quite easily use smithsofwashington.co.uk (yes American readers, *our* Washington is where *your* George's family – and name – originated).

It is the availability of suitable domain names on pertinent suffixes that is one of the primary reasons for Greek, Latin or totally made-up words being used by new companies and those launching new subsidiaries or re-branding themselves in the marketplace. Such words are unlikely to have been registered as domain names. Another alternative – if the money is available – is to buy an existing generic name around which your entire business, website and brand will be built. In this scenario, the company name will effectively become the *brand* – and so in all of the discussion and research into a suitable brand name, the availability of domain names will be a significant factor in that decision-making process. For the company that trades globally (or plans to), there is the additional problem of having the domain name available in a selection of suffixes – indeed, perhaps *every* suffix. It is in this latter scenario where the domain name question is inextricably linked to the business strategy of the proposed venture. For example, when expanding into international markets, the key marketing problem is 'do you localize or standardize your marketing mix?' Allied to this in the digital age is 'do you localize of standardize your web presence?' Though the issue is somewhat more complex than I am suggesting here, the normal practice would be that localized website would sit on the local suffix of the domain name, and standardized sites would be based on extensions of the 'home' domain – usually a .com.

It is for the localized web presence that the 'invented' word comes into its own. Examples of such names include:

- The name chosen for the web presence representing an ensemble of European airlines: opodo. Apart from reading the same upside down (a good idea for a passenger jet?), I can only guess that this made up word had not been registered as a domain name anywhere in the world. It certainly has no logical connection with flying or air transport.

- After a rather acrimonious split from its 'parent' (Arthur Andersen) some years earlier, in 2001 Andersen Consulting decided to make that break even more obvious by re-branding itself as *Accenture*. Although the PR at the time suggested the name was derived from 'accent on the future', I can't help but think that the lack of trademarks and domain names anywhere in the world for the made-up name played a part in the decision-making process.

A postscript to the suggestion of using made-up words as company names would be to avoid deliberate misspellings. Much of the reason why is covered in chapter 3.17 where I address text and SMS abbreviations in domain names, but I'll sum it up in one word. Unprofessional.

3.06 CHOOSING THE *RIGHT* DOMAIN NAME FOR A BRAND

If the *domain* name is to be the *brand* name, then the criteria for each must be considered separately as well as synchronized to create a name that serves both purposes equally well. This book is full of all things 'domain name' therefore that aspect is covered, so let's take a quick look at the basics of brand names.

The concept of branding is reputed to date back to the ancient Egyptians, who would mark their cattle with a unique image so that strays could be identified as belonging to that owner. The contemporary marketer operates much the same way, seeking to distinguish a product or service from the competition and create a lasting impression in the mind of the customer. Online, the domain name is the equivalent of that mark on the cow's hide.

Issues to consider will include things like:

- The personality of the organization – Google, for example sounds a bit 'off-the-wall', non-conformist, whilst Microsoft is more formal (it is not by accident that these two companies, like many others, reflect the personality of the individuals who formed them)

- Is there to be a logo, and if so will the brand name be part of it? If this is the case, then the aesthetics of the brand/domain name will be important

As for the actual name, many of the issues raised in the previous section on creating the right domain name that is also the company name apply. Most significant are the issues of names being created from:

- Invented words (Xerox)

- Initials (IBM, B&Q)

- Founder's names (Johnson & Johnson)

- The benefit offered by the brand (Toys 'R' Us, U–Haul)

- Generic names that are divorced from the organization or its products (egg.co.uk, moonpig.com – respectively, a bank and greetings card provider)

With the notable exception of the invented word when it comes to selecting a suitable domain name, all of these options for a *brand* will face the same problems described in previous sections that addressed the selection of a company name.

DOMAIN NAMES IN PRACTICE

parked up and going nowhere?

The following generic names are all 'parked' – and presumably making money from the ads featured on the pages – but I can't help thinking they could be used better by different owners: card.com, cloth.com, clothing.com, cool.com, fight.com, gamble.com, home.com, join.com, men.com, pay.com, personal.com, plan.com, queen.com, store.com and super.com. Given the necessary marketing budget for a new online-only business, I would have though the asking price for some of these would be worth a slice of that budget.

3.07 CHOOSING THE *RIGHT* DOMAIN NAME FOR A PRODUCT

This is, perhaps, the easiest of the domain name decisions because the domain for a product should match the name of the product itself. Not withstanding any grammatical issues (such as possessive apostrophes and question or exclamation marks), any difference between product and domain name will dilute the brand of that product.

Whether you are a global corporation like Procter and Gamble or an owner-manager working from home, you should have trademarked all of your product names and so it is that name that you should register as a domain name. An added advantage to having existing trademarks is that you may have the *right* to those domain names.

However, if you are a small manufacturer that trades only in your own country or region, the problem of existing domains in the name of your product might be more difficult – something that is common if your product carries a generic aspect to its name eg 'excellent carpet cleaner'. If you cannot resort to the law, then other options might be available. Simply adding a country identifier to the name might work; excellentproductuk.com for example. Or maybe use hyphens if your product name is more than one word, excellent-product.com, for example. However, if you have a new product that is yet to be named, then the availability of a suitable domain name should become part of the decision-making process. As with company and brand names, this is – I think – one of the main reasons for invented words being used as product names.

3.08 CHOOSING THE *RIGHT* PROMOTIONAL

DOMAIN NAME

Such has been the acceptance of the Internet as a medium for marketing that it is unusual for a contemporary *offline* ad not to feature the domain name or URL of an associated website. Whilst many ads simply include the domain name of the product, brand or organization (eg nike.com) others feature the web address of a site that developed as part of a specific promotion or campaign. As in a number of sections of this chapter, the decision on a promotional domain name concerns far more than the domain. In this case the domain name is just *part* of a promotional – normally advertising – campaign, something that would be strategic in nature and include other media (and associated costs) in their execution. This is, therefore, another section where the domain name decision is (almost) made for you in that the domain name is simply the name of the campaign – and campaigns are normally given a specific, and unique, title. This means that it would be unusual to find the *right* domain name to be unavailable. These titles are most often a short phrase or term, so whilst their domain names would never work as a company or brand name, simply registering the domain name of the campaign title is perfect. It is worth noting that one objective of the ad campaign will be to make the (potential) customer remember the tagline (catch phrase) of the ad (eg Nike's 'just do it'). It is not, therefore, a great leap of faith to expect that phrase to produce a website when typed into a browser.

If matching the domain name to the tagline is easy, then the choice of the tagline should consider the domain name it will become – again, there is a bit of chicken and egg here. There are two essential considerations:

1. Choose a phrase that has not been registered as a domain name. Be extra careful to check multiple suffixes. You don't want to run a campaign tagline for a kiddies toy on the .co.uk suffix, only to later discover a foreign company has used the same (or similar) term for a not-so-kiddy-like product and have registered the .com version of the phrase.

2. Make sure the phrase can become a domain. The following list of examples includes Pedigree's 'what's your dog's thing?' They just about get away with whatsyourdogsthing.co.uk, but two apostrophes and a question mark have had to go absent without leave. Promotional domains tend to ignore the hyphen, presenting the phrase as all-one-word. As with domains for other purposes, the use of numbers is also problematic, though registering the full spelling and numeral versions can overcome uncertainty.

Rather than attempting to list every nuance and detail that may crop up in promotional domain name decisions, perhaps the best route is for me put forward my opinion on a number that I have seen over the years. Because I live in the UK, they all come from Europe-centric campaigns. However, if you are elsewhere in the world do not be put off by this – it is the concept I am reviewing, not the geographic implications.

So here you go, in no particular order:

- Let's start with a good example of an imaginative domain name as part of an integrated communications mix – that of MG Cars a few years ago (when MG still existed!). They ran a campaign based on the results of a having a group of enthusiasts test their MG ZT+190 against a comparable BMW. The results were very favourable for MG and they built a promotional campaign around those statistics. The domain name of the website for the campaign? mgbeatsbmw.co.uk. Nice one.

- In September 2005, Procter and Gamble's Old Spice made an aggressive integrated marketing push to attract 18 to 26–year–old males by launching an ad campaign supported by four interactive and heavily branded websites. One TV ad showed a sexy girl dancing in a nightclub, with the tagline 'When she's hot, it's sexy. When you're hot, you stink.' The second ad actually parodied the first. The tagline being the same, but the video was of a rather overweight Lothario in leather trousers doing what he thinks is a sexy dance. The two associated websites sat on whensheshot.com and whenyoustink.com. Full marks on domain name choice for these. The same goes for the third site in the campaign; 'Music in the Zone', which could be found on musicinthezone.com. However, another Old Spice site – Old Spice Racing – was found on the brand's primary domain – oldspice.com. Oldspiceracing.com was registered, but by someone else who has seized the opportunity to put a pay per click ad site on it. I would have thought the might of the P&G lawyers could have recovered the name and so keep a consistency across the four campaigns.

- Other sites use phrases that describe the product rather than represent a tagline. For example, softonyou.com is the website of the Nouvelle Marketing Department of Georgia-Pacific GB Ltd. A public relations site for Nouvelle toilet rolls, much of the content is aimed at children and their education on environmental issues. With the exception of a page detailing current promotions the site is non-commercial, so why the commercial – and global – .com for a UK campaign? Given the nature of this site, I would suggest that it is an ideal candidate for the .info. Like the product itself, softonyou.info is more gentle on the user. Footnote to this: Typing softonyou.co.uk into your browser returns 'page cannot be displayed', yet the domain name has been registered by of Georgia-Pacific GB Ltd. Why not have it made live and redirected to the website? It would cost very little – quite possibly nothing, but anyone typing the domain name with .co.uk into a browser in error would still have found the Nouvelle website.

DOMAIN NAMES IN PRACTICE
The biter bitten?

In April 2004 the organization People for the Ethical Treatment of Animals (PETA) arranged to 'borrow' the use of a domain name from its owners who were selling the name, but not using it on a website. A good idea from PETA. Even better when you consider the domain – meat.com.

- Perhaps we should not be surprised that sleepbetter.co.uk is the Horlicks website. That we are *not* surprised is testament to the Horlicks brand – though sleepbetter.com returns a 'cannot find server or DNS Error' message. Caught dreaming on that domain perhaps?

- The idea of using phrases as domain names to describe the website is not restricted to commercial entities. For example, givingupsmoking.co.uk is part of the UK National

Health Service's effort to encourage people to stop smoking and targetingbenefitfraud.gov.uk aims to catch cheats. But why does one use the .gov.uk suffix and one the .co.uk? Perhaps another opportunity for .info? At least the .gov suffix links the campaign to the government and so makes it non-commercial, whereas the .co.uk in the smoking ad could be perceived as being a commercial company selling stop-smoking aids. As a footnote, maybe someone had a word in their ear on this one as the domain name subsequently redirected traffic to smokefree.nhs.uk.

- The questionable use of suffixes is continued in a UK initiative to encourage people to find out about all aspects of drugs – 'Talk to Frank'. The domain name used in TV adverts is talktofrank.com. Yet the site's content is repeated on talktofrank.co.uk (not something that search engines take too kindly to, they consider it to be search engine spam). The issue is this; as the site is a UK site, why not use the .co.uk address in offline promotions? The TV advert on which I saw the domain promoted came across as a quasi-governmental initiative, but given the subject it is perhaps sensible for the organizers to stay away from the .gov.uk suffix (the campaign tries to avoid being 'official'), but .com is for US (global) commercial entities. Perhaps .org.uk would have been a better choice.

- Amongst those who don't really get the nature of promotional domain names is Pedigree, who advertised their dog food with the tagline 'what's your dog's thing'. However, typing whatsyourdogsthing.co.uk into your browser took you to www.uk.pedigree.com/dogslife/dogthing.asp – a members-only section of the parent website devoted to the 'what's your dog's thing' promotion.

- Huggie's promotional domain name 5xstretchier.com redirected users to huggiessuper–flex.com. Again, why no website – or even web *page* – on 5xstretchier.com? That aside, this name is problematic with both the use of a number (as discussed previously) and the use of 'x' to replace 'times'. However, brickbats turn to plaudits because 5timesstretchier.com, fivetimesstretchier.com and fivexstretchier.com all redirect to huggiessuper–flex.com. Top marks for that at least.

- In the UK a common term for starting out in home ownership is to 'get your foot on the property ladder', so the domain name footontheladder.com was a good choice for Mortgage Point Ltd's radio ads promoting 100% mortgages to first time home buyers. Though again, why the global .com?

- Used as part of 'Making Britain Healthier' – a campaign led by a group of private hospital and medical insurance companies – was the domain makingbritainhealthier.com. Although the domain name might suggest an altruistic website about food and exercise, the website is – effectively – an ad for the services offered by the sponsors. However, we should give them their (marketing) due. If I were searching for health advice and this domain name appeared near the top of a search engine results page I would be tempted to click on it. Need I also add that .com for a domain name with 'Britain' in it is dubious – perhaps the .com was perceived as being less commercial than .co.uk?

- The website on food.gov.uk is that of the Food Standards Agency (the content is more like what you might have expected to find on makingbritainhealthier.com). As .gov.uk names are only available to government departments, generic words [on the .gov.uk suffix] are widely available for government-sponsored promotions. This is a good use of that availability.

- This Lynx deodorant ad campaign suggested that using said antiperspirant made a man more appealing to women than – amongst other things – Ben Affleck. Hence the tagline 'spray more, get more', and the domain name spraymoregetmore.co.uk. The site featured video clips of the ads, including those too raunchy to appear on prime–time TV – an excellent example of how websites can be used as an integral element of any brand building strategy

- The domain name goneabitnoodles.com hosted a zany site that reflected the similarly off-beat nature of the TV ads for Peperami Noodles. In this case the *actual* domain name is zany simply because it is carries the nonsensical name of the campaign.

- A campaign from furniture retailer IKEA was aimed at 'encouraging a better balance between life at work and life at home'. As with other campaigns from this retailer, the whole thing was delivered with tongue firmly in cheek with its website sitting on lifeoutsidework.co.uk.

- To re-launch Head & Shoulders shampoo into a new market, P&G's campaign included NFL player Troy

Polamalu (who has distinctively long hair), complete with a related website at troytacklesmore.com – but for reasons known only to themselves, the domain redirected to headandshoulders.com/en_US/troytacklesmore/default.jsp Harrumph.

- No great problems with the concept of developing a website to enhance a promotion with the tagline 'food deserves better', this time from Knorr (part of Unilever Bestfoods UK Ltd), but the domain name fooddeservesbetter.com looks odd with double 'o' followed by double 'd' – I had to *double-*check after I had typed it on this page! At first glance, it even reads 'food served better'. This is one example where – as the domain name person – I might have questioned the tagline right from its first conception, a time when an alternative phrase might have been devised. Note that I address the issue of domain names seeming to read differently to what they actual are in chapter 4.02).

- Another example of a tagline that does not get a tick in the domain name box is 0for10.co.uk from Barclaycard. This domain name was used as part of a 'zero percent interest for 10 months' credit card offer. Remember what I have already covered with regard to numbers? Well zero adds another dimension in that it has other terms to describe the number. The domain 0for10.co.uk worked, but none of the following did: Ofor10.co.uk, 0forten.co.uk, zerofor10.co.uk, zeroforten.co.uk naughtfor10.co.uk, naughtforten.co.uk. A saving of around £60, Barclays shareholders must have been delighted.

- This one is a little different in that the organization's main website sits on a promotional domain name. Featured on TV ads for their products, lovethegarden.com is the domain name of the UK web presence of the Scotts Miracle-Gro Company. The site offers advice to gardeners, and appears to be a portal-type site that is sponsored by company rather than the company's home page (there are logos and links to information about the company's main products on each page). The give-a-way comes in the contact email address – consumerenquiries@scotts.com. Scotts being the parent company, with scotts.com being the North American website. Interestingly, it is also presented in portal style, this time for grass and lawn care.

- I include energy drink Lucazade's goneabitlara.co.uk and breath mint Tic Tac's shakeyourtictacs.co.uk because they were amongst the first ads to use the tagline of the promotion as a domain name. Both worked well as the ads were humorous – as are the taglines and domain names. Sadly, both URLs now return a 'Server not found' message – what a wasted opportunity to have the promotion live on. If nothing else, they should have kept the domain live and have it redirect to the main brand site.

- Here's one I had to give up on. This domain was on a TV ad, but I wasn't' really watching and I just caught the ad's drift – and didn't really hear the URL clearly. I wrote down what I thought was the domain name, based mainly on the term as it was spoken in the ad – which I thought was 'meatelicious.com'. However, I tried all kinds of spelling for the phrase, it being the combination of meat and delicious. Now perhaps I am being stupid, maybe I miss-heard or just lost the plot. But, and it is a big *but*, I never found the website. So who is the loser – me or the advertiser? The moral is – if the domain name isn't obvious, folks won't find the website.

You will note that I have compiled this list over a number of years. As the majority are linked to a promotional campaign that has a limited time frame, there is the question of what to do with the domain when the campaign is over (who knows where the domain might be noted, site bookmarked or listed on a search engine?). I'll not go into too much detail as the problem is more *marketing* than it is *domain name* – but as an online marketer I would say you have three options:

1. Post a landing page that explains the site's originally purpose and add links to other organizational web pages

2. Redirect the domain to your primary site – or other similar promotions, perhaps via a landing page

3. If the site is informational in nature, re-write the content so that it is 'timeless', as opposed to being directly related to the promotional campaign.

If you value your brand, the following are NOT options:

• Just leave the site as is – with an out-of-date message

• Delete the site, so leaving a 404 'gone away' message

• Let the domain name lapse, allowing a domainer to put up a site and so benefit from *your* campaign

Also worth adding as a postscript to this section is that the concept of promotional domain names is not universally accepted in the marketing community. Their opponents put forward the argument I suggested in the earlier section on company domains, that is; having different organizational and promotional domains divides the marketing effort. This can mean divided brand loyalty and increased costs. However, I would argue that in the case of promotional domains, the savvy marketer can actually *double* the advertised product's exposure in that the viewer might go online looking for the product by name or by the tagline of the ad. This *should* – if the campaign's marketing is fully integrated – result in the promotional message reaching the potential customer which ever route they follow.

3.09 CHOOSING THE *RIGHT* DOMAIN NAME FOR A MICROSITE

I thought long and hard about even including this section because a microsite falls very much between the promotional site and the landing page – the subjects of the previous and next sections. There is also an issue with the definition of what a microsite is. In my book *Key Concepts in e-Commerce*, I say the term is generally used to describe one of two types of web presence: (1) where the organization's objectives can be met by the content of one web page, or (2) a website that is on a different domain to the organization's primary site because it serves a different purpose to the rest of the web presence. In terms of microsite domain names, the first of these issues is covered by the guidelines for organizational names, and in the second the website described is likely to be covered in one or other of the sections of this chapter – 'promotional', 'landing page' or 'unexpected', for example. However, I will offer an analysis of the domain name side of things in what I think is an example of a microsite.

In September 2005 the Hard Rock Cafe chain opened a new outlet in Times Square, New York. As part of an impressive promotion for the new cafe a microsite was developed on its own domain name. This was a departure from the norm for Hard Rock, which has all of its other outlets, hotels, casinos, events, memorabilia and merchandise on hardrock.com. However, the launch of the new cafe was considered significant enough to have its own domain name – rocktimessquare.com. There are three points of interest on this:

1. Why not hardrocktimessquare.com? This would be the obvious domain name, but the promotion had a distinct emphasis on 'rock' and so the choice makes sense – particularly as the URL was featured heavily on promotional literature – with the microsite being the only way customers could enter a competition to win a trip to the opening night in New York. Given the cost of the marketing overall, however, a few dollars to register and redirect hardrocktimessquare.com seems a bit short-sighted. If nothing else it would have prevented any kind of scam being perpetrated on the domain.

2. After the launch the domain name defaulted to hardrock.com/rocktimessquare. Given the policy of having all content under the same domain name, this is understandable. However the pages were not updated until some two months after the event (ie they talked of the launch event in a future tense). During the aftermath of such a massive promotional campaign that featured the rocktimessquare.com domain I would have thought that content could have been developed for a page on that domain – perhaps featuring images and a narrative of the events surrounding the opening of the new outlet.

3. Some four years after the event the domain rocktimessquare.com defaults not to the webpage of the Times Square venue of the company, but a 'cafe news' page. Although that page includes a link to a 'cafe locator' facility, it seems to me that anyone who typed in, or clicked on a link for rocktimessquare.com would rather be taken to the designated web page for the New York cafe.

3.10 CHOOSING THE *RIGHT* DOMAIN NAME FOR A LANDING PAGE

Normally seen as an integral – and essential – element of the sales conversion funnel, the landing page has a specific role to play in moving the potential customer towards whatever action will meet the objectives of the ad to which they have responded. This objective could be anything from an online purchase through newsletter sign–up to the directions to the nearest bricks-and-mortar store that carries the advertised product. A landing page is one specifically developed as the place where users are directed when they respond to a promotion. This is not the same as the promotional domain name (which will host a purpose-built website), but a 'response' page on the organization's main website. Such a page would sit on the main domain name, something like atrusingbusiness.com/specialoffer, atrusingbusiness.com/freegift or even simply atrusingbusiness.com/tv, with the file name pertaining to the promotion.

Whilst registering domain names for specific ads is an option, beware of being too free with the registration of new domains for landing pages. Indeed, this is one of the only sections of the book where I advise *against* registering a new domain name. Having the landing page on one domain and the 'shop' on another (probably the organization's primary domain) may create uncertainty in the mind of the customer, with them perceiving the company to be untrustworthy. If this is a potential problem, the way round it is to ensure that the landing page is clearly branded as being part of the 'parent' organization.

There is, however, one aspect of online advertising where the domain name is an essential element. This is the 'display URL' – that part of a search engine or network ad's copy text that tells consumers where they will go if they click on your ad. For this type of online advertising a promotional domain is most definitely *not* an option. All of the major engines and network ad providers enforce the following rules with regard to the format of display URLs:

- The top level domain of the display URL must match the top level domain of the ultimate landing page

- The display URL can be a sub–domain eg advert.atrustingbusiness.com

- The display URL can be an indexed page eg atrustingbusiness.com/advert

So whilst a new domain name could be registered simply for an advertising campaign, for the majority of search engine and network ads it is your organization's primary domain name that is the most suitable for such ads. However, you can use the second/third level names for such ad campaigns, so some of the stuff you learned in chapter one will be useful. Although second level names can be used if your search engine/network advertising is limited, I would suggest the use of indexed (file) pages as being the best option where multiple landing pages are used. Without going into too much detail, to be effective, each ad should have a 'customized' landing page, which means each needs its own URL – not really an viable option for second level names if you have 1000 different ads running at any given time.

3.11 CHOOSING THE *RIGHT* DOMAIN NAME FOR A COMMUNITY WEBSITE

This kind of website can be divided into two; the commercial and the non-commercial. Although I would always argue that the *right* domain name is the *best* domain name, it has to be said that if the website is a simply place for like-minded folk to meet and discuss their mutual interest or hobby – and not to make money – then the domain name does not carry the same significance as for a commercial site. In such instances, I would follow my 'company' advice (chapter 3.04 & 3.05) and suggest registering the name of the community as the domain name. Even if your community has a generic term included in it (quite likely, actually) combining the place in which it exists or its 'legal' designation (association, society etc) should address that issue. If other similar groups do exist or your community is 'virtual' rather than geographic, try .net or .org suffixes – both suggest a lack of commercial concern and so might better attract the target audience. For example, the 'Springfield Model Boat Society' could use springfieldmodelboatsociety.org, or the 'Model Boat Society' modelboatsociety.net.

The *commercial* community site is one that has been developed by an organization as part of its marketing communications strategy, but is not part of its corporate site – though the site might represent an online presence for a brand or product. The lovethegarden.com website of the Miracle-Gro Company I featured in the promotional domain names section (chapter 3.08) is an example of this concept. For the commercial community site, the domain name guide is a combination of that for the non-commercial and the promotional site – in other words register the domain name that describes what the website is about – Miracle-Gro's could just as easily have been gardeninghintsandtips.com, for example. For commercial sites I would stick to commercial suffixes (eg .com), though this might be another good application for a generic term on a .info suffix – modelboats.info for a model boat manufacturer, distributor or offline magazine, perhaps.

3.12 CHOOSING THE *RIGHT* DOMAIN NAME FOR A GEOGRAPHICAL DESTINATION WEBSITE

I'll start this section with a confession – I have made up the term *geographical destination website* because I could find no suitable term to describe those websites that are about a *place*. As with community sites (in the previous section), these sites can be commercial or non-profit – though in my experience the latter are rare, with even 'amateur' sites hosting ads to generate income. The main problem for the publisher of the destination website is that all geographical names have long since been registered – and, as with generic terms, domains like london.com, newyork.com are extremely valuable.[6] However, salvation is at hand by way of adding an adjective, verb, descriptive phrase or even question to the name of the place. Examples might include:

visitathens	allofboston	allaboutnewyork
singaporeonline	paris365	tokyoontheweb
exploreneworleans	whyvisitseatle	whattoseeinsydney

The domain name can also be easily made to match the purpose or objectives of the site, for example:

hotelsinlasvegas	wheretoeatindublin
madridrestaurants	mexicocarhire

I suspect that at least some of the above have been registered. However, not only will these – I hope – give you food for thought, but it is unlikely that every combination of region,

---

[6] As an aside, the organization I worked with back in the day had quite a few geographic domain names and I had a number of interesting conversations with entities such as City Councils and Chambers of Commerce who claimed they 'owned' the name of their location.

city, town, village or locale and descriptive adjective has already been registered on the various suitable suffixes.

DOMAIN NAMES IN PRACTICE

make it clear

I saw this on an ad 'sticker':

> **Visit**
>
> **Birmingham**
>
> .com

What would you type into your browser: birmingham.com or visitbirmingham.com? It's the latter, but *my* first thought was the former.

Something of a footnote to this section is advice for the local organization that is in some way 'selling' a destination elsewhere. For example, consider this: I am a UK travel agent who specializes in putting together trips from the UK to Toronto. Obviously, toronto.ca and toronto.com will be long-since registered – but what about putting my Toronto-vacations website on toronto.co.uk? Conversely, the Chicago Tourism Bureau might put a website targeting UK citizens on visitchicago.co.uk, with similarly targeted – and translated – websites for other countries (and suffixes) around the world.

3.13 CHOOSING THE *RIGHT* DOMAIN NAME FOR A BLOG

Although the term 'weblog' was first used by Robot Wisdom in December 1997, 2005 was the year in which blogging came of age as an online marketing tool (the term 'blog' was introduced in 1999 and the practice dates back to the early 1990s). Moving beyond the 'traditional' blog – a kind of personal journal on subjects that interested the writer – *commercial* blogs are generated by organizations as a form communication to reach potential markets. As with websites, it is possible to host your company blog with a provider that offers free hosting – but you do so at your peril. Having a weblog address ending in something like blogspot.com or typepad.com might be OK if the blog is made up of your own personal content, but for the organizational blog this is unprofessional. In similar fashion to website hosting, I say register your own domain name and either pay for the hosting of your own blog or simply use one of the blog providers that allows you to have your own domain name (my blog is hosted by blogger.com, but the URL is alansinternetmarketingblog.com, not alansblog.blogger.com).

As far as name selection goes, the obvious choice is to add 'blog' to your existing domain and register it using the same suffix as the original. For example, atrustingbusiness.com becomes atrustingbusinessblog.com. Or, if you can host the blog on your server, simply use a third level domain on your own – blog.atrustingbusinesss.com. If you are using your blog to generate interest in a market – in the same way as the community website described earlier – go for the generic word or phrase with 'blog' added. From the example I used in the earlier community domain name section, gardeninghintsandtips.com would become gardeninghintsandtipsblog.com. Or, as not every generic word or phrase with 'blog' added has been registered, you could try gardeningblog, gardenblog, gardensblog, gardenerblog or gardenersblog. The suffix is not so important because users are most likely to access the blog pages through a newsletter, RSS feed, search engine or your own website – making memorizing the correct suffix unnecessary, though as a rule of thumb use the same suffix as your main website. Who knows, one day we might have a .blog suffix?

3.14 CHOOSING THE *RIGHT* DOMAIN NAME FOR THE UNEXPECTED OR UNWANTED

In business, things go wrong. They might be relatively small things that are sorted in-house. Or they might be bigger things that impact on the organization and its environment. Although the two are fairly close relatives, the *unexpected* and *unwanted* present the organization with different domain name demands.

The unexpected is a problem because it is just that – unexpected. The unwanted is, you guessed it, unwanted – but it is not unexpected per se, so at least you can plan for it. Registration of domain names in these circumstances will be part of any public relations (PR) effort that seeks to address problems created by an unexpected or unwanted happening. The first issue to address is whether you feel it necessary to register a designated domain name or simply use your main domain with a sub-directory (eg atrustingbusiness.com/unexpectedproblem). I think I would favour a dedicated website on an assigned domain for a number of reasons, not least that it divorces your brand website from the 'problem' of the moment – and don't forget the 'problem' web pages will stick around on the search engines' indexes for a while. A site independent of the main site will also help with tracking the metrics of the consumers' response to the problem. More intangibly, a dedicated domain might be perceived by affected consumers as being a serious attempt to address whatever issues have been raised by the 'problem'. Let's now take a look at the unexpected and the unwanted specifically.

The unexpected can't be planned for because you don't know what it is, so when it happens you need to move fast. An example might be a poorly worded evaluation of your product on a TV consumer-advice programme or a news story that unfairly presents your organization, brand or product in a bad light. More serious would be something like a production error making it necessary to withdraw a product from sale. Although domain names can be registered and made live in a short space of time, it can take 24 hours or more for the domain to be listed on servers around the globe. This being the case, the IT department or your hosting provider should be made aware that a live domain name might be needed in a hurry and prospective plans put in place. As the unexpected cannot be predicted you can only prepare generic *types* of name. However, if the construction has been agreed before any event occurs, at least time will not be wasted on its discussion when the worst does happen. Obviously, it depends on your product, brand and market, but I would look at things like productnameproblem, productnamerecall, productnamefault or if the problem is less serious, productnameadvice. None are perfect, but then neither is having a situation that requires such action. A .info suffix might add to the perception that the site is there to address a problem, rather than a more commercial .com or .co.uk which might smack of marketing.

The unwanted is the event that you try to avoid, but have to be prepared for its happening. In some circles this is known as disaster recovery, but the PR folk would rather call it contingency planning. The term might be softer, but not as appropriate because it fails to suggest the urgency of *disaster recovery*. Whilst I concede that unexpected problems are also unwanted, I class these events as being more serious that simply saving [marketing] face in the press. An obvious example would be something that has caused loss of life – an air crash or ship sinking for example. In these cases the major organizations have plans in place to cope with such a disaster, so having a 'dormant' site sitting permanently on a suitable domain name is not beyond the realms of forward thinking. Obviously, the speed of corporate reaction is a factor – there is no need to have a domain sitting ready on a server it is takes the organization 48 hours to get a press release out. However, when a US Airways plane crashed on the river Hudson in January 2009, the story was on Twitter and the images on YouTube before the major news services had run the story, let alone the airline react. So in this social media-driven world, organizations must be prepared to act quickly – and what better than a 'tweet' that directs everyone to a purpose-developed website on an appropriate domain name less than an hour after the incident?

An example of preparing for a negative event comes from the GAP retail organization. In August 2005 they closed down their gap.com, oldnavy.com and bananarepublic.com websites for 'scheduled site improvements'. The wisdom of closing down the sites for two weeks at the height of a back-to-school shopping season was the subject of some debate, but that discussion is for a different book (my opinion – why couldn't they build and test the new site on a 'hidden' sub-domain then simply transfer it over to the main servers?). Of domain name interest, however, is that the 'under construction' message that appeared when gap.com was typed into a browser sat on the domain gap-underconstruction.com.

Some forethought seems to have made in the domain names department, if not in GAP's e–commerce executive office.

Footnote #1 to this narrative – reviewing the revised gap.com site I noticed that clicking on the 'about GAP' link takes you to gapinc.com. Nice idea – I like 'corporate information' to be on a different site to the online shop.

Footnote #2 to the GAP story – as of May 2006, some nine months after the site redesign, the gap–underconstruction.com web page was still live – with the rather cryptic message 'thank you, now you'll be the first to know when you can start shopping again'. Why not simply redirect to the gap homepage? Or given that gap–underconstruction.com was used for oldnavy.com and bananarepublic.com as well, give a brief commentary on why the page exists 'this domain name was used as a temporary measure whilst our sites were re–designed' and a list of links to sites the user might be looking for (including the aforementioned gapinc.com).

3.15 CHOOSING THE *RIGHT* DOMAIN NAME FOR AN EMAIL ADDRESS

Before I suggest what you *can* do, I'll start with something you must *not* do. And that is, never, ever, ever, use the following as a business email address:

* The address given to you by your Internet Service Provider (eg @aol.com)

* An address of one of the many free services available (eg @googlemail, @hotmail, @yahoo)

Going back to my earlier example neither sunderland.welding@serviceproviders.emailservice or sunderland_welding@yahoo.com present the organization in a professional light – remember my comment about first impressions in the book's introduction?

DOMAIN NAMES IN PRACTICE
defining names in email addresses

I suppose that sooner or later it will appear in some 'protocol' guide or other – but for now take this advice as good practice. If you are putting staff names before the @ in your company domain names, separate their given and family names by a full stop. Hence, my 'work' address is alan.charlesworth@. I think this is the most logical set up as it identifies the addressee by their full name. No full stop can work, but as with domain names, there can be issues when two words run together. Similarly, initials can be problematic – recently, I had to look twice at the email of one Harold Andrew McBride – hamcbride@. That the company web page referred to him as 'Harry', made this email address even more confusing.

The best email system – and so choice of email addresses – is where your organization's domain name is linked to what is known as a POP3 (post office protocol version 3) account. If you have ever worked for a company where all staff email addresses are theirname@thecompanydomainname and they can all access their 'company' email from any Internet-connected computer anywhere in the world, this is most likely to be POP3 account. However, such systems are usually maintained by the organization's IT department – or out-sourced service providers. Whilst all reputable domain name registrars will offer a POP3 option to your domain hosting service, for many (very) small businesses, setting up your own POP3 email account can be a concern. Whilst I would always suggest it is the best path, there is an acceptable option. This is where you have emails to your domain name forwarded to your 'free' account. For example, if you send an email to email@alancharlesworth.eu, that message will arrive in my alan.charlesworth@gmail.com inbox. You can also have outgoing messages from the gmail account carry your domain name email address. In googlemail, for example, click 'settings', 'accounts', select 'add another email address' and then enter (in this example) email@alancharlesworth.eu. Finally, make sure the 'reply from the same address the message was sent to' option is selected. It is as simple as that – effectively, your googlemail account is transformed into an email account for your new address. Note that I have used gmail as an example because I actually have the set-up described above, other free accounts also offer a similar facility.

As with domain names, there are both rules and advice for what can and cannot be used as an email address. Technically, the receiving server can be set up to accept almost anything prior to the @ sign in an email address. I mention this only in passing – you should stick to A to Z and the full stop to avoid confusion. I remember having to think twice when I first saw an ampersand (&) used by American TV broadcaster in the email address of their news anchor team. I forget the exact names, but it was something like gillian&peter@abc.com. If I was a bit confused, would others not be also?

Even numerals can cause bother. I once came across a small business that had two employees with the same forename, so their email addresses were dave1@ and dave2@. Whilst it was common practice within the company to avoid confusion by referring to them as 'one' and 'two' – as an email address ... definitely not. Even beyond the lack of professionalism in this practice, there is the problem of verbally communicating the address – is that dave2@companyname.com or davetwo@companyname.com?

As with its use in URLs (see chapter 1.13), the underscore should also be avoided in email addresses – for two significant reasons. Firstly, the underscore is not part of any language, making it alien to any combination of characters or words, and secondly when it appears on a website, the web protocol default is for it to be underlined – making the underscore 'disappear'.

In the early days of the web it was often considered to be a sensible option that if your domain name was long and/or complex then a separate name be registered for email addresses. At the time, the idea had some merit. Using my previous example of the fictitious Sunderland Fabrication Welding Ltd, their web presence is unlikely to be a decisive element in attracting new contracts, therefore www.sunderlandfabricationwelding.co.uk is probably quite acceptable for their website. However, twenty-nine character domains do not make for snappy email addresses – and if I worked for the company it would take an extra long business card to fit on all 16 characters of my full name before the @ of @sunderlandfabricationwelding.co.uk. Although the name is (relatively) easy to remember, the more characters there are to type, the more the chance of a mistake being made. The solution *was* to register an acronym or a shortened version of the company name. In the case of my fictitious welding company in Sunderland, sales@SFW.co.uk is relatively easy to remember, and difficult to misspell. Alas, this is not an option because SFW.co.uk has already been registered – and this is the reason why the practice has died out. No three or four character combinations on all the popular suffixes remain unregistered and so not available to use as email addresses. So my made-up company would be stuck with alan.charlesworth@sunderlandfabricationwelding.co.uk – maybe they could only recruit people with short names!

DOMAIN NAMES IN PRACTICE
sent – but not received

If you spell a domain name wrong in a browser you know straight away that you've made a mistake because you get either a '404' message or a different website to the one you wanted. Get an email wrong, however, and you might never know. Certainly, most systems will let you know if your email has bounced, but what if your 'wrong' address exists? What if that confirmation of an order went to sales@acb.com instead of your sales@abc.com?

I recall the organization I worked with had the domain sunderland.com – and I was designated to receive emails that were sent to any @sunderland.com address. I received dozens of emails where the writer thought they were sending a message to someone at golf apparel manufacturer, Sunderland Golf.

Note that as I am such a wonderful chap, I forwarded them all to @sunderlandgolf.com – despite the fact that the company's owners frequently demanded we give them 'their' domain name. They argued the name was rightfully theirs as the firm had existed since 1966. We politely pointed out that the city of Sunderland in the North East of England was granted a charter in 1179!

If you do decide to go for using a different domain name for your email, make sure that your ISP sets up the 'email domain' so that if it is typed into a browser the surfer is redirected to your website – and also that emails addressed to either domain name reach the same person (eg sales@sunderlandfabricationwelding.co.uk and sales@sfw.co.uk both go to the same person or department). This is not difficult to do and should not cost much money (if any). If your current ISP doesn't know what you are asking for, find a new ISP.

And finally, as with domain names, email addresses are not case sensitive. People's names, being proper nouns, should always be spelt with capital letters. And yet I have not used any capitals in the examples above. The reason is simple. I know email addresses are not case sensitive. You know email addresses are not case sensitive. Unfortunately, the majority of people do not, and to introduce capital letters in the address may confuse the less well informed (I always smile when I hear people giving their email address as – for example – 'ted dot baker at mydomain dot com, that's upper case 'T', lower case e–d, dot upper case 'B' ... and so on. I don't have the heart to correct them). Hopefully, anyone reading this book in a few years time will wonder what the fuss was all about, because by then use of appropriate upper and lower case in email addresses will be common practice.

DOMAIN NAMES IN PRACTICE

a question of email-address-influenced credibility

Example #1

Whilst writing this book I looked around at companies that facilitate self-publishing, so I put "book self publishing" into Google, and clicked on a sponsored link for www.diggorypress.com. The top of their website's home page read:

DIGGORY PRESS PUBLISHERS: To contact us: Email: meadowbooks@hotmail.com or diggorypress@hotmail.co.uk

These people might well be the greatest self-publishers on earth, but would I trust sending my slaved-over manuscript to a company with hotmail email addresses?

Example #2

An email with a job vacancy arrived in my inbox a while ago. The company might well be a legitimate company offering real opportunities, but considering *only* the two featured email addresses, how credible is this sender?

From: Warren Connell <h_daniella@hotpop.com>

GET A JOB! --- *the job details were listed here*

Regards, Cargo Transport : group

groupcargotransp@aol.com

Warren Connell, the author/sender, doesn't seem to have his own email address as he uses that of 'H Daniella', who has a 'hotpop' account. The company, the Cargo Transport Group, uses an AOL account as its business email account. To apply for a job you have to submit a CV. That's a lot of personal information to give to someone you have never met and have only the content of an email message on which to base your trust.

3.16 CHOOSING YOUR PERSONAL DOMAIN NAME

In earlier sections we have looked at instances where the company owner's name is part of the domain name, indeed, there will be times when the owner's name *is* the name of the firm – particularly in the case of consultants. For those occasions all the rules of choosing a domain for businesses apply, but in this section I want to concentrate on domain names for *personal* use – that is non-commercial – be it for a website or email. Whilst some might feel this whole subject is too narcissistic to consider, I would argue the opposite. If nothing else, it is recognising the way the Internet *has*, and will continue *to*, influence the society in which we live. For the really sceptical, perhaps you should consider the concept simply to stop someone else registering your name as a domain name and putting un-flattering content on it.

So why register your name as a domain name? Well, the main issue is that you can control the content of any website that is hosted on it. That might be anything from your life history, through a full CV/résumé to just your email address. Naturally, if you are private person this is still not going to be high on your list of life's priorities. But if you have any web presence at all – be it on facebook, your employer's website, myspace, youtube or friends reunited – then why not have something about you where you have total control of the content? I would even go further and suggest your own website will become an essential part of our lives in years to come – in much the same way as people now cannot do without a contact phone number (mobile or fixed-line). Indeed, what better email address than @yourownname? Could it even be the case sometime in the future that our credit ratings might be higher because of the credibility factor of having our own website on our own domain name? Think I'm exaggerating – or even being paranoid? Do you think that employers (or their agents) looking to recruit a new member of staff don't already put the names of applicants into Google? Or businessmen and women don't check up on individuals before arranged meetings? Well, they do – and how impressive do you think an appropriate website on that name coming up top of the SERP is? It is certainly better than those pictures of you on a drunken night out which are on your friend's facebook site (note that I have been telling students this for years, I hope some listened). It strays from the point slightly as the emphasis is on the service provider not you, but I know of managers of top-end hotels who have staff search on customers' names before they arrive at the hotel. The concept is that they might learn something about the individual or family that will help staff make their stay better.

For many, if not the majority, the advice included in this section is some years too late – for all combinations of common names have long-since been registered (particularly on the .com suffix) usually because they are the names of businesses *somewhere* in the world. And I cannot really explain *why*, but .com is the suffix to have for your personal domain name. Certainly in the UK, having a .co.uk suggests you are a legal entity of some kind – as would be the case in other countries that use 'commercial' suffixes. This perception also includes the .eu and .asia domains. Similarly, a .org suggests 'organization'. However, your personal domain is perhaps one where some of the 'novelty' suffixes can work – .cc perhaps. Don't forget also .net and .info – the latter particularly if you are putting together a web page that will appeal to prospective employers.

So what to do if the combination of your given and family names have already been registered on the .com? Well, if you have tried the appropriate suffixes try them again with a hyphen between the two names. Common for those entering the acting fraternity is to differentiate yourself from others with a similar name (it is an actors' union requirement) by including the initial of any middle names. Be prepared, however, to use this initial all of the time if the domain name that includes it is to be any use. Taking this notion to an extreme, you could always invent a middle initial to differentiate your domain from others. In this regard I am always reminded of the movie *North by Northwest*, where Cary Grant's character Roger O Thornhill comments that the 'O' in his name stands for 'nothing', and intimates that as an advertising executive he needs to stand out from the norm. It would certainly have helped me get a .com domain if when I started out on my publishing career I had called myself Alan O Charlesworth – though in this case it sounds a bit Celtic (ie O'Charlesworth), so perhaps an 'H' from my mum's maiden name would have been better (Hmmm, Alan H Charlesworth actually has a ring to it).

I am, of course, being somewhat light hearted here, but where your name might become your brand name these things are worth consideration. For example, a neighbour of mine trades under his own name, but as it is the same as a famous film star he really struggles with his search engine rankings. For those of you who agree that the future might see us all have our own domain name, could it be that domain name availability might become part of the baby name choosing process, with a middle name added if the .com has already gone? Don't scoff too much at this suggestion, the baby's name as a domain name is already a popular christening present – and who wouldn't want their child to grow up to be famous? If that is the case, how pleased will your offspring be if they already own theirname.com?

DOMAIN NAMES IN PRACTICE'
tel everyone your contact details

A novel new domain is one that does not allow advertising on its web pages, making it unattractive to domainers and cybersquatters.

The .tel domain name does not allow pay-per-click advertising because it will not host websites. The domain's web pages contain only contact information which will be sent to phones and computers that look up the domain. The restricted page content is uploaded via the registrar rather than by file transfer protocol (FTP). Is it worth having? Well, it costs very little, so ROI is not really an issue. I think it is good for individuals (for private or commercial purposes), but then their website should contain the same information. The key to its success – or otherwise – will be how highly they list on the search engines.

3.17 USING TEXT AND SMS ABBREVIATIONS IN DOMAIN NAMES

It could well be an age thing – I am well past my youth – but as a generalization, I would advise that abbreviations found commonly in text messaging should be avoided in domain names. However, as these have (unfortunately) crept into more general usage, there are exceptions to this rule. In this case those exceptions will come where the target market is willing to accept abbreviations because it is the language they use everyday – teenagers, for example. Perhaps the most acceptable is the use of numbers in place of words. The two most popular being '2' and '4' in place of the prepositions 'to' and 'for' respectively and the use of 'u' instead of the pronoun 'you'. Interestingly, perhaps the most common example of these combine '4' and 'u' to replace 'for you' – as in phones4u and lawyers4u. Both of these are the actual names of the organizations – so their domain names follow suit.

As I have already covered in the section covering the use of numbers in domain names in chapter 3.02, a significant issue comes where the domain name is communicated verbally. The answer comes in registering the name with both the number and the word. This is fine if the domain name is based on the company, brand or product name where some legal recourse is available against squatters, but if you are using a number because the word version has already been registered then you have already lost out. By definition, this can create problems for two businesses that trade online on product4u.com and productforyou.com as customers will be easily confused.

> **DOMAIN NAMES IN PRACTICE**
> **when numbers don't add up**
>
> Phones4u have their website on phones4u.co.uk. Also redirecting to that name are phones4u.com, phonesfouru.co.uk and phonesfouru.com. Interestingly, the latter reflect the translation of the character '4' to the word 'four', whereas in the literal meaning of the name '4' is an abbreviation of 'for'. However, phonesforu.com and phonesforu.co.uk are not owned by Phones4u.
>
> Another company that uses '4' in the same way is cash4gold.com – who ran TV adverts in which the voice-over said; 'go to our website on cash4gold.com, that's cash, the number four, gold, dot com'. Need I add a comment?

Other abbreviations and substitutions exist in the txt wrld – and some have evolved from times long before Twenty First Century teenagers thought they had discovered the misspelt word as being cool. Luv for love, for example, or replacing cks with x. And what about Australian rock band INXS (in excess) – their name dates back to 1979. Similarly, replacing the plural 's' with a 'z' (eg kidz) has been with us for a while. However, despite their use being around for decades, I would advise that using any 4u-type terms or replacing 'cks' with an 'x' in your domain name is to take a risk in any market place other than that of the SMS generation. It would need to be rather enlightened grand parents who would consider buying a £2000 glass structure for growing plants from a website called greenhousez.com, for example. Similarly – and although I think I can see where they are coming from – I feel the credibility of the insurance-advice company kidzclaimz.co.uk is compromised by their name. My final example of questionable use of such abbreviations is a haulage company based in my region. Ferguson Transport – presumably after discovering that another company had registered fergusontransport.co.uk – elected to go with fergytrux.com. Now perhaps this is how the company is known within the logistics industry, but wouldn't the CEO of any organization looking to allocate an essential distribution contract for its products prefer to deal with a company whose website uses a domain name made up of words that can be found in a dictionary? Note that at the time of writing fergusontransport.eu, ferguson-transport.co.uk and ferguson-transport.com were all available.

DOMAIN NAMES IN PRACTICE

do you know what u are doing?

August 2006 saw the UK's Advertising Standards Authority (ASA) ban an ad that featured a domain name which caused problems for respondents. There is an element of irony that the Home Office's website for the Child Exploitation and Online Protection (CEOP) Centre failed to consider their domain name registration policy (if there is one!) before going live online. Their promotional domain name was thinkuknow.co.uk – and the issue was with the use of the 'u' for 'you'. They probably thought it appealed to the *yooff* market – but problems arose in that the CEOP ad ran on the radio. The voice–over simply referred to the website as 'thinkuknow.co.uk' – and, of course, loads of folk typed in thinkyouknow.co.uk.

Unfortunately for the CEOP, this took users to a parked domain which featured a whole host of links, some of which were to the exact kind of sites that the CEOP was warning children and parents about.

3.18 A FEW TRICKS WHEN ALL EVERYTHING ELSE HAS DRAWN A BLANK

If you have got this far in the book and I have still not helped to solve your domain name selection problems, this could be the segment for you – though I suspect some of you may well have skipped straight to this section!

For those who are at a total loss and are unable to come up with a domain name for your organization or business venture, the following 'last-hope' advice comes in the form of the scientific and the artistic. As a marketer, I much favour the latter, but computer science can offer some help, so I'll start with that.

If you are struggling to come up with a suitable domain name – presumably because the most suitable has already gone – a number of online 'domain name generators' exist which produce a list of suggested, and available, domain names based on keywords entered. In other words, if you sell a certain product or you trade in a specific market, you input terms that are related to that trade or market. As the resulting list is computer-generated, I am sceptical about their value, but they can serve as a kind of brainstorming aid. For example, I tested one such site's system by researching their offerings for two separate keywords; 'Sunderland' (say, for a portal website about the city), and 'e-marketing' (perhaps for a new consultancy business).

'Sunderland' produced a number of novel returns that served only to reinforce my scepticism of these devices. All on the .com suffix, they included; sunderland-java, sunderland-attic, sunderland-s and sunderland-goblin. The only one in the list of around 30 suggestions that had any semblance of value as a domain name was 'sunderland-search', *perhaps* something that could be used for a portal for the city. However, more suitable for that application would be search-sunderland, which was available but not included in this list.

The search on 'e-marketing' was equally dubious. Suggestions included; e-marketing-gang, dyna-e-marketing, recluse-marketing and exemplifying that computer driven search can lack any common sense, eprivatetreaty and the somewhat baffling e-bootlegging! On the plus side, however, e-marketing-room and e-marketing-people might be used by a new business offering e-marketing services. Perhaps worth noting is the prevalence of hyphens in these 'suggestions' – yet the generator site was based in the USA.

Whilst tools such as the one described above are designed specifically to generate potential domain names, other applications exist that can be adopted to help in brain storming for possible names. One such type of online tool (often free, Google's is) is that which tracks and records the keywords used in search engines to find specific sites. Whilst the purpose of these reports is related to search engine marketing, they can offer the domain name hunter something also.

As an example, the following terms were published by Hitwise (hitwise.com) as being used by shoppers who were looking for the website of UK fashion retailer 'Next'. The first search term is obvious: 'next'. Another two are URLs:

- www.next.co.uk

- next.co.uk[7]

Two other terms used by searchers have links with the Next offline entity, those being

- next catalogue
- next directory

This is not a surprise as Next Directory is the name of Next's printed catalogue. The final four of the 'next' search top ten, however, all offer something to a would-be online clothes retailer who is looking for a domain name. They are;

- next clothing
- next shop
- next clothes
- next online

Obviously, the word *next* is a no–no if you want to avoid legal action, but if it fits, try adding 'clothing', 'clothes', 'shop' or 'online' to the name of, or brand used by, your offline business. For example, a fashion boutique called 'Prior' might use priorclothing, priorclothes, priorshop, or prioronline.

Although this example pertains only to fashion retailers, you can easily repeat the process using as a search term the name of your main competitor or brand leader in the marketplace. Similarly, most of these online tools also allow users to check on the terms used by search engine users to find specific information, so you could conduct the research based on generic product terms or services. For example, if you

---

[7] Quite why so many people type 'www.next.co.uk' into a Google search box rather than directly into their browser is an issue for a different book.

are selling garden-furniture, put those words into the tool and see what the analysis says. You will be surprised to see some of the terms searchers used in their quest for information, so perhaps your analysis might come up with a term that hasn't been registered as a domain – or at least give you something to think about.

If that is what science has to offer, what about the intangible – the *art* of choosing a domain name? The following are in no particular order of quality or importance – but somewhere in these examples there might be *something* that gives you an idea for the right domain name for your website, brand, company, product or organization. By this stage of the book, I hope that there is no need to remind you that different suffixes to your preferred option might be available for all of the suggestions – so don't just think of .com!

- Make the domain name a combination of the target market segment and the product or service being offered – studentloans is an obvious application of this concept, but the options are limited only by the number of product and target customer combinations. Perhaps worth noting with this route is the use – or not – of the possessive 's' in any of these combinations. For example studentloans could just as easily be studentsloans. Whilst this increases the potential for suitable domains, some terms really do need the possessive 's' for them to be logical – gardenergloves, for example, doesn't make the same sense as gardenersgloves. This opens up another possibility if the description of the customer (gardener) is also a verb (to garden) – which is often the case. In this example, gardeninggloves actually makes more sense. Don't forget, of course, all of these can use a hyphen instead of being all one word – gardening-gloves might actually be preferable as the hyphen splits the two 'g's. Another variation on this theme would be to reverse the words and add a preposition – glovesforgardening or glovesforgardeners, for example.

- In generic product-based names, take a lead from offline retailers who have for years been inventive in naming their shops. The use of the abreviation for et cetera – shoesetc, for example. Or perhaps for an up–market site, use the full word, shoesetcetera (why up-market? Your clientele has to understand the word, some demographic groups might not realize that etc is an abbreviation). Interestingly, shoesetc has been registered on most suffixes, shoesetcetera on none. Another option is to use a short phrase. Consider 'and much more', for example. What about shoesandmuchmore for the ladies accessories store? (as I write, it is currently available in all US suffixes). Don't forget also that with the examples given, and any others you might come up with, there is always the use of the hyphen if the first choice is gone. In some cases, the inclusion of a hyphen can actually help the term make more sense – for the ladies accessories shop for example, shoes-andmuchmore, the hyphen replaces a comma in emphasizing that the sentence addresses two product areas. Try saying it out loud, as in; 'we sell shoes, and much more' – or as a domain name, what about 'wesellshoes-andmuchmore.com?

- Another tip from offline retail is the *world* concept. Dolls, for example, could be sold on worldofdolls or dollsworld – although the latter works better if the product can be presented – and still make sense – without the possessive apostrophe, furnitureworld or vanworld for example. As with all multi-word domain names don't forget the hyphen. In these cases it is (almost) grammatically acceptable to use a hyphen, so its use in a domain name is this context is ideal – furniture-world or van-world, in the previous examples.

- Also for the established offline retailer, is to add a 'descriptor' to the company name. This could be as easy as adding 'online' (sunderlandtoysonline), '365' to reflect that the Internet shop is open every day (sunderlandtoys365) or 'direct' to suggest the product is available *direct* to your home rather than only in a physical store (sunderlandtoysdirect). Each of these can also be used with 'sales' to emphasize the purpose of the site – sunderlandtoysonlinesales, for example. Perhaps you could state the obvious by adding 'website' (sunderlandtoyswebsite) – though prefixing the term with the definite article will emphasize the standing of the business by employing 'the' as an adjective (thesunderlandtoyswebsite), this is something that can work with a common name (thealancharlesworthwebsite) where the emphasis is on the website being the official one in a sea of fakes. Going back to the first 'descriptor' – *online* can also be used with a myriad of generic terms. This can be particularly effective for 'interest' sites, be they commercial or not – tomatoesonline or gardeningonline for example. Note however that reversing the words does not have the same effect. For example, onlinetomatoes suggests the fruit is actually being grown in some kind of virtual environment!

- Sometimes *simple* works. Prefixing a generic combination with the definite or indefinite article can make the name distinctive or might even have the site appear more important in the eyes of the potential customers. Using 'the' might add a little *something* to a domain name, remember, 'the' is also an adjective – theonlineshoestore, for example. On the other hand, aclifftopbedandbreakfast sounds a little less pretentious than theclifftopbedandbreakfast.

- Prefixes to the product name can also work, with a variety of options being available. Try a verb (lovefootball) or an adjective (allhondaparts). An extension to this theme is the use of an adjective to describe the target customers (keenanglers or dedicatedgolfers). For places or hobbies you could 'discover', 'visit', 'think' or 'explore' virtually any location or subject. For the more forceful sales site you could try prefixing the subject with a verb so that the domain name becomes almost a command or instruction – the obvious one for an online shop being 'buy' – buyshirts, buytables etc, or buyshirtsonline perhaps. Other *softer* verbs are more suitable when associated with the objectives of the website – words like 'seek' or 'find' go nicely with tourism or gifts and sound more like a request than a command. Or consider using a phrase instead of a single word – 'look for', 'look at' or 'look to', for example. If the website is meant to reflect the essence or culture of something (perhaps a place or practice) the verb might be something that reflects a more intangible act – 'think' (thinksafety) or 'feel' (feelfit), for example, or add the definite article to make the subject more explicit (feeltheheat).

- Another possibility for a sport, pastime or hobby (and in some circumstances a place), would be to prefix them with 'enjoy'. Whilst combinations such as enjoysquash or enjoychess have limited applications for an online environment (they just don't sound right), a website that extols the virtues of a city or region as part of its promotion to potential visitors would sit comfortably on 'enjoy' – enjoyglasgow, for example. The use of verbs in this way must be considered with caution – and due deference paid to not only the *actual* definition of the word, but people's *perceptions* of what they mean. For example, where 'enjoy' implies that visiting the place or playing the sport would be a pleasurable experience, terms such as 'like' or 'appreciate' just don't work – we don't normally visit a city on holiday to *like* it. But on the other hand, we do *appreciate* fine art or architecture – so, used in context, the possibilities are limited only by your imagination.

- A prefix is not the only way to go – don't forget about giving the subject a suffix. If the application suits, try adding a noun – 'things', for example, gives fishingthings, swimmingthings and so on. Taking this a stage further would be to insert 'and' in much the same way as suggested earlier in the shoes example. The online fishing accessories store could become fishingrodsandthings. Of course, *things* might not work for some products or organizations, so get out the thesaurus and look up other options. Perhaps 'kit' might be better for sports products (tenniskit), 'gear' for pastimes (walkingear) or 'equipment' for more complex pursuits (divingequipment).

- Along the same line is to use an adverb or adjective to narrow the range of products being made available by using words like 'just' or 'only' in combination with either the product (justsneakers) or the target market (onlytoyotadrivers).

- As mentioned in previous sections, promotional domain names can also make use of dates within the phrase – remember people always write a year in numerals (ie '1956', not 'nineteen fifty six'), so the numerals versus in-full issue for numbers doesn't apply. In some circumstances promotions lend themselves to the inclusion of a year as they tend to be time specific. Such practice also makes the use of long-gone generic words viable, something like football2009.com, for example. Although some campaigns are almost self-designating (Athens 2004 or Germany 2006, for the Olympics and World Cup respectively, for example), a promotional campaign for a holiday resort might be something like 'ibiza2010bethere'. An issue with this route is that, obviously, the domain and any site hosted on it will go out of date on the first of January of the following year. However, with a little forethought this can be used to the organization's advantage.

Take my home-city's annual International Airshow, for example, whose web presence is on the local council's sunderlandevents.co.uk. I would not only have a dedicated website for the airshow, but update the domain name each year – sunderlandairshow2009 and so on. The *why* is all about search engines and using the web to meet the needs of users (I call it Internet marketing). Take the 2009 show for example, which featured a fly past by a rare Vulcan bomber. If the website on sunderlandairshow2009.org had a user-generated content element that allowed visitors to upload their photos and videos of that display, aircraft enthusiasts anywhere in the world typing "Vulcan bomber pictures" or "Vulcan bomber video" into Google would get the site. As the years go by – 2009 was the 21st Sunderland International Airshow – each website would feature high in Google searches, and so the city would gain brand recognition.

As with every chapter, this section does not profess to give all the answers – but I hope it has given you something to think about.

CHAPTER 4

where and how to show off your domain name

I have decided to put this chapter at the end of the book because both sections are relevant to all of the various types and applications of domain names that have been covered throughout the earlier content.

4.01 WHERE DO YOU FLAUNT YOUR DOMAIN NAME?

The obvious answer to this is *everywhere* – or at least *anywhere* potential customers might see it. This would include any or all of the following:

- On all corporate stationery, including headed note paper, invoices, receipts and – in particular – business cards.

- Adverts, in all media. This refers to company domain names in general as well as promotional names registered for specific campaigns.

- All promotional literature. This includes not only direct marketing letters, flyers and so on, but product catalogues, trade show hand-outs and any other kind of printed materials.

- Promotional give-a-ways. This is an infinite list of virtually any item that can be given away, from pens and note blocks to sports bags. A personal favourite is mugs as they tend to get used rather than stuck in the bottom of a draw (or worse still, thrown out) and they often stand next to the user's computer, just where you want your domain name to be.

- Where appropriate, on the products themselves. This has obvious limited applications – few businesses can put their domain name on the side of aeroplanes as do Virgin and easyJet, for example. Putting your domain name on a piece of furniture would be unlikely to impress customers (though it could be included on a label on the underside). However, 'flymo.com' on the side of a lawnmower instead of just 'flymo' would not be unreasonable.

- Product packaging, including labels and boxes, cartons etc. Note that in these circumstances there is consideration of each product having its own domain name. If this is the case, the 'corporate' domain should also be included.

- Point of sale materials used in both retail and wholesale outlets. Note that in the latter the URL might be that of the section of the site that is relevant to the B2B trader rather than the end-user.

- Company vehicles. Trucks and vans obviously, but cars can also be suitable in some circumstances. The boot of the CEO or MD's Mercedes is a bit tacky, but if the nature of the business means there are a number of staff using cars to perform their duties then that would be a consideration. Estate/realty agents would be an example.

- Employee's clothing. Once again, the CEO or MD probably gets away with it and does not have their Armani outfit spoiled by having 'atrustingbusiness.com' emblazoned across the shoulders. However, polo shirts, overalls and work coats can actually be enhanced by a discrete – but readable – domain name. I could add baseball caps and tee shirts here, but although employees *might* wear them, they are better listed under promotional give-a-ways.

- On anything related to any sponsorship the organization might be involved in. This would include event banners, press releases, literature or other promotional material.

- On any materials or tools used in the course of the day-to-day operations of a business. For example, scaffolding and vehicles on a construction site.

- As a footer on all general communications emails (that is non–direct marketing emails). However, considerations include:

(i) Do you make it a hyperlink? I'm inclined towards no. It's a personal thing, but I think that they look aesthetically wrong as the link shows up blue, bold and under-lined – unlike the rest of the message that is (normally) black, not bold, and not underlined. To me, the hyperlink just comes across as in-your-face advertising, which might be in contrast to the actual message being transmitted. Should anyone want to go to your website they can 'cut and paste' the URL into a browser.

(ii) Do you use the domain name rather than a URL? My concern here is that the email might be about a specific product or subject that has its own page or section within a website. Putting the domain name only will take the reader to the home page of the site, and not the page of the subject in question (eg company.com or company.com/emailsubject).

Now that you know *where* your domain name should be seen, make sure you read the next section to read *how* it should be seen.

DOMAIN NAMES IN PRACTICE
do as we say, not as we do

In November 2004 I had reason to check out the American Marketing Association (AMA). Naturally, I looked online, and started by typing in the obvious domain names and suffixes. I had to give up and revert to a Google search, which revealed that the domain name of the American Marketing Association is marketingpower.com. Excuse me, *marketingpower* – where did that come from, a domain name generator from chapter 3.18?

I can excuse them missing 'AMA' on the various suffixes (well, almost – the AMA has been around since 1937, did they not think of registering a domain name back in the mid 90s?), but what about americanmarketingassociation?

At the time of writing (August 2009) the .com (for americanmarketingassociation) was available for purchase, .info and .org (seemingly) owned by speculators and .net hosted a website that had 'American Marketing Association' across the top of the homepage, but is nothing to do with that organization – making it (I would have thought) suitable for a recovery claim from the AMA.

4.02 AESTHETICS; WHY IT MATTER HOW YOUR DOMAIN NAME LOOKS?

First impressions can be crucial. Online, the company's domain name may influence how a potential customer might perceive the organization (poor domain name = poor company, good domain name = good company to do business with). But domain names are not only used in internet browser windows, they are seen offline as well. They appear on stationery, on business cards, company literature, on vehicles and on adverts – in fact, in every other medium to the Internet. For these, we must consider the aesthetics of the name, that is, how it will look when presented on all of these media.

Primary in the aesthetic presentation of domain names is the use of upper and lower case to help clarify meaning by identifying separate words within that name. Indeed, if you take only one thing from this book, this is it: domain names are NOT case specific. When used to type a URL into a web browser, domain names are NOT case sensitive. Both offline and online, they can be presented in lower, upper or sentence case[8]. When used offline, therefore, the aforementioned yorktoys.co.uk is presented as YorkToys.co.uk. In this particular case this is not a major issue, but with other names it can have great significance. Let me use an example from my own experience.

A company that specialized in organizing and hosting trade show exhibitions of child-related products was called

---

[8] Technically, a server can be set up to recognize upper and lower case characters in a domain name, but it is universal practice to set them up to accept both. Indeed, it is so common that many technical staff are not aware the option exists.

Children's Exhibitions Ltd. (they have since ceased trading). So they registered their business name as a domain name. Stationery bearing the name was already ordered when I pointed out how their name would look in print:

childrensexhibitions.co.uk

Because of the way we identify outstanding words within a series of letters, at first glance the phrase 'children sex' is prominent, or even 'children's sex exhibitions'. Not what the business was hoping to promote. The solution was relatively simple. In print the name could be presented as ChildrensExhibitions.co.uk. An alternative would be to use a hyphen between the two words of the domain name; Childrens-Exhibitions.co.uk. Even without the capitalization of the words this would still read childrens-exhibitions.co.uk. Note that in chapter 1.04 I make reference to the use of the hyphen. Whilst many practitioners in the USA are vociferous in their defence of the all-one-word rule for domain names, surely examples such as this show that there are exceptions to the rule.

It is not only 'smutty' word associations that can cause problems when multi-word domain names are presented offline. When consecutive words end and start with the same letter where they join will always attract the eye, but three letters the same looks like a misprint. For example, in the run-up to the ban on smoking in the work place in the UK, a TV campaign promoting the date of the event used the domain name smokefreeengland.co.uk for its online presence – notice how SmokeFreeEngland.co.uk looks much better. This example brings to the fore another issue. As a country's name is a proper noun it should always be capitalized to be grammatically correct – it can seem very strange to see words we associate with being capitalized in lower-case. This is particularly true of acronyms – fbi looks wrong, for example, it is always presented as FBI.

DOMAIN NAMES IN PRACTICE

schoolyard humour, but not funny in business

Other examples of lack of forethought when registering domain names include the following.

Sex is a popular theme in this regard – like the betting advice site, oddsexchange.com (odds exchange) and the site facilitating skill-swops, expertsexchange.com (experts exchange). Of course, the essence of this cautionary tale is that you should avoid any kind of rude misinterpretation. So it is that MP3 download site mp3shits.com (mp3s hits), and a database of contacts called 'Who Represents' that becomes whorepresents.com online both raise a giggle. An example of how a word you would never sub-divide takes on a life of its own when it is part of a domain name is the site that helps therapy seekers – therapistfinder.com (therapist finder). And what about the tourism site for the Iberian peninsula – ChooseSpain.com which becomes a masochists' holiday destination – ChoosesPain.com? Finally, just to show that wordsmiths can get it wrong too, the pen might be mightier than the sword, but as a domain name penismightier.com says something else. Note, at time of writing, all of these domain names had *genuine* sites on them.

Depending on the media, the marketer can use colour or tone to differentiate words within a domain name. This is perfectly acceptable if the marketer has control over any reproduction. An example comes from the star-studded 2005 campaign against world poverty. Its domain name was presented on various media as **make**poverty**history**.org.

I hope the examples I have included above will have convinced you of the importance of domain name presentation in offline environments, but if you need more evidence the following is a selection of the domain name examples I have listed throughout the book. When writing the text, I made the decision to deliberately present every domain name in lower case. Here is a sample of some as I wrote them in the text – with how they *should* be portrayed alongside each.

all lower case	best aesthetic presentation
alancharlesworth.eu	AlanCharlesworth.eu
europesbestkeptsecret.com	EuropesBestKeptSecret.com
twitter.com	twitter.com (the brand uses all lower case in its name)
bbcmotiongallery.com	BBCMotionGallery.com bbcMotionGallery.com (this name just doesn't look *right* in any version)

all lower case	best aesthetic presentation
taxreturnadvice.com	TaxReturnAdvice.com
men.com loans.com pizza.com fly.com	Men.com Loans.com Pizza.com Fly.com (It can be the case that with short, one–word domains, capitalizing the first letter *can* make the presentation seem unbalanced – what do you think?)
seo.com	SEO.com (it's an abbreviation of 'search engine optimization')
boots–plc.com	Boots–plc.com (this breaks my 'capitalize abbreviations' rule because plc is normally presented in lower case – I don't know why)
suzuki–gb.co.uk	Suzuki–GB.co.uk (as an abbreviation for Great Britain, GB is always presented in upper case)
suzukimarine.co.uk	SuzukiMarine.co.uk
yescarcredit.net	YesCarCredit.net
newcastleairport.com	NewcastleAirport.com
magnum7sins.com	Magnum7Sins.com follows the rule, but Magnum7sins.com looks better
tripadvisor.com	Another example where the brand name uses all lower case (eg tripadvisor) – so TripAdviser.com is wrong

all lower case	best aesthetic presentation
domainnames.com	DomainNames.com
yorktoys.co.uk	YorkToys.co.uk
alanstoys.co.uk	AlansToys.co.uk
stationtaxismanchester.co.uk	StationTaxisManchester.co.uk
hallamsofimmingham.com	HallamsOfImmingham.com or HallamsofImmingham.com (the 'of' causes a problem here as the upper case 'O' takes the eye)
northeastmobility.co.uk	NorthEastMobility.co.uk
whensheshot.com	WhenShesHot.com (whilst I approve of the campaign from which this comes, it is a good example of where the missing possessive apostrophe looks odd)
softonyou.com	SoftOnYou.com (I would normally advise that prepositions be left in lower case – as in titles – but in this case SoftonYou.com looks like two words instead of three)
footontheladder.com	FootOnTheLadder.com (an example of capitalizing every word looking better)
talktofrank.com	TalktoFrank.com (an example of capitalizing only the key words looking better)
makingbritainhealthier.com	MakingBritainHealthier.com

all lower case	best aesthetic presentation
vavavoom.co.uk	VaVaVoom.co.uk (another example where all lower case might be better. Perhaps the capital Vs take the eye too much)
mgbeatsbmw.co.uk	MGbeatsBMW.co.uk
spraymoregetmore.co.uk	SprayMoreGetMore.co.uk
goneabitnoodles.com	GoneABitNoodles.com (the 'a' makes this one tricky – perhaps an example of when bold and/or colours would help eg **GoneABit**Noodles.**com** or Gone**ABitNoodles.com**)
lifeoutsidework.co.uk	LifeOutsideWork.co.uk
fooddeservesbetter.com	FoodDeservesBetter.com
goneabitlara.co.uk	GoneABitLara.co.uk or GoneaBitLara.co.uk (notice how the indefinite article [a] causes problems – so much so I might say stick with all lower case)
atrustingbusiness.com	aTrustingBusiness.com (the lower case indefinite article looks better)
rocktimessquare.com	RockTimesSquare.com
springfieldmodelboatsociety	SpringfieldModelBoatSociety
visitathens	VisitAthens / visitAthens (with place names being proper nouns, use of the lower case for other words *can* work quite well)

all lower case	best aesthetic presentation
allaboutnewyork	AllAboutNewYork allaboutNewYork the 'a's make this one tricky
tokyoontheweb	TokyoOnTheWeb (the capitalized 'on' and 'the' looks poor – but better than the double 'o' in the all lower case version)
wheretoeatindubai	WhereToEatInDublin
whyvisitseatle	WhyVisitSeatle whyvisitSeatle (notice how the combination of 'y' and 'v' causes problems)
whattoseeinsydney	WhatToSeeInSydney (in this one, the two 't's make the first word 'whatto')
hotelsinlasvegas	HotelsinLasVegas (could it be that the lower case 'in' works for this particular venue as it creates the word 'sin'?)
wheretopartyinberlin	WhereToPartyInBerlin
gardeninghintsandtipsblog	GardeningHintsAndTipsBlog
gap–underconstruction.com	GAP–UnderConstruction.com (the GAP brand uses upper case letters in its brand name)
thinkuknow.co.uk	thinkUknow.co.uk (another rule-breaker, this time the use of 'u' to replace 'you' causes problems, in this example the upper case 'U' emphasizes that the term is three words)

In chapter 3.18, I use a lot of examples for when everything else has drawn a blank – why don't you try 'capitalizing' them as an exercise? I am assuming that I don't need to add that suffixes should *always* be presented in lower case.

Finally, it is worth adding a quick word on presentation of domain names in adverts in offline media. I agree with P&G in its presentation of website URLs on their adverts. The TV advert for Ariel, for example, simply says 'ariel.com'. They do not bother, you will note, with the 'www'. I will accept the argument that there will always be newbies to the Internet who do not recognize a domain name, but I feel these are few and if they cannot identify a domain name, they are hardly likely to access the website online. I think that a simple name-dot-suffix is aesthetically clear and clean, and gets across the message. This is an evolutionary thing. In 1998 I remember strongly advising a major UK retail organization against printing the domain name of their new website on all of their stationery and carrier bags including the http:// before the www. They said that people would not know what 'www.theirname.com' was. I gave them a similar argument to that above – that people who were likely to access the website would know the URL without the http:// – but they were insistent. For several years – until they saw the light – I cringed every time I saw one of those carrier bags. The web has, however, moved on still further.

An evolution of domain name presentation might, therefore, look something like this example of the fictional business; the Baltimore Opera Hat Company, which has the domain name baltimoreoperahatcompany.com.

Back in '96 it would have been:

http://www.baltimoreoperahatcompany.com

Within a couple of years the http:// was gone:

www.baltimoreoperahatcompany.com

By the turn of the century upper-case characters were being used:

www.BaltimoreOperaHatCompany.com

Next to go was the www:

BaltimoreOperaHatCompany.com

By 2006 the Internet was so ubiquitous that the mere mention of a domain name suffix denotes – to most people – a website address. Regular web users also know that there are no gaps in a domain name when it is typed into a browser. Therefore, if I were running an ad for a product that was targeted at a web-savvy market segment, I might simply put:

Baltimore Opera Hat Company com

Note that in this one I haven't even included the full stop – the dot – before the com. Omitting the full stops is already common when verbally communicating the double-barrelled suffixes such as those used in the UK – simply referring to the suffix as 'co-uk', so do we need to read them in print? Realistically, I would say the answer is probably 'yes we do' for most markets, but then who knows what the future will bring?

You have now made it to the end of the book – congratulations!

Has it been useful? Insightful? A waste of money?

Or maybe I got something wrong?

Let me know on email@AlanCharlesworth.eu

When necessary, I will keep the various aspects
of the book updated on its own website:

AlanCharlesworth.eu/domain–names

And if it is any interest to you, there's lots more e-marketing
stuff on my website: www. AlanCharlesworth.eu – or should
that be:

Alan Charlesworth eu